LOGICS FOR ARTIFICIAL INTELLIGENCE

ELLIS HORWOOD SERIES IN ARTIFICIAL INTELLIGENCE

Series Editor: Professor John Campbell, University of Exeter

COMPUTER GAME-PLAYING: Theory and Practice
M. A. BRAMER, The Open University, Milton Keynes
IMPLEMENTATIONS OF PROLOG
Edited by J. A. CAMPBELL, University of Exeter
PROGRESS IN ARTIFICIAL INTELLIGENCE
Edited by J. A. CAMPBELL, University of Exeter and L. STEELS, Vrije Universiteit, Brussels
MACHINE INTELLIGENCE 8: Machine Representations of Knowledge
Edited by E. W. ELCOCK, University of Western Ontario and D. MICHIE, University of Edinburgh
MACHINE INTELLIGENCE 9: Machine Expertise and the Human Interface
Edited by J. E. HAYES, D. MICHIE, University of Edinburgh and L. I. MIKULICH, Academy of Sciences, USSR
MACHINE INTELLIGENCE 10: Intelligent Systems: Practice and Perspective
Edited by J. E. HAYES, D. MICHIE, University of Edinburgh and Y.-H. PAO, Case Western Reserve University, Cleveland, Ohio
INTELLIGENT SYSTEMS: The Unprecedented Opportunity
Edited by J. E. HAYES and D. MICHIE, University of Edinburgh
MACHINE TRANSLATION: Past, Present and Future
W. J. HUTCHINS, University of East Anglia
AN INTRODUCTION TO PROLOG
L. SPACEK, University of Essex
AUTOMATIC NATURAL LANGUAGE PARSING
K. SPARCK JONES, University of Cambridge and Y. WILKS, University of Essex
THE MIND AND THE MACHINE: Philosophical Aspects of Artificial Intelligence
Edited by S. TORRANCE, Middlesex Polytechnic
LOGICS FOR ARTIFICIAL INTELLIGENCE
R. TURNER, University of Essex
COMMUNICATING WITH DATA BASES IN NATURAL LANGUAGE
M. WALLACE, ICL, Bracknell, Berks
NEW HORIZONS IN EDUCATIONAL COMPUTING
Edited by M. YAZDANI, University of Exeter
ARTIFICIAL INTELLIGENCE: Human Effects
Edited by M. YAZDANI and A. NARAYANAN, University of Exeter

LOGICS FOR ARTIFICIAL INTELLIGENCE

RAYMOND TURNER

Professor of Computer Science
University of Essex

First published in 1984
and Reprinted in 1985 by
ELLIS HORWOOD LIMITED
Market Cross House, Cooper Street, Chichester, West Sussex, PO19 1EB, England

The publisher's colophon is reproduced from James Gillison's drawing of the ancient Market Cross, Chichester.

Distributors:

Australia, New Zealand, South-east Asia:
Jacaranda-Wiley Ltd., Jacaranda Press,
JOHN WILEY & SONS INC.,
G.P.O. Box 859, Brisbane, Queensland 4001, Australia

Canada:
JOHN WILEY & SONS CANADA LIMITED
22 Worcester Road, Rexdale, Ontario, Canada.

Europe, Africa:
JOHN WILEY & SONS LIMITED
Baffins Lane, Chichester, West Sussex, England.

North and South America and the rest of the world:
Halsted Press: a division of
JOHN WILEY & SONS
605 Third Avenue, New York, N.Y. 10158 U.S.A.

© 1984 R. Turner/Ellis Horwood Limited

British Library Cataloguing in Publication Data
Turner, Raymond
Logics for artificial intelligence. —
(Ellis Horwood Limited series in artificial intelligence)
1. Artificial intelligence
I. Title
001.53'5   Q335

Library of Congress Card No. 84–19810

ISBN 0–85312–713–1 (Ellis Horwood Limited)
ISBN 0–470–20123–1 (Halsted Press)
Typeset by Ellis Horwood Limited.
Printed in Great Britain by R. J. Acford, Chichester.

Q
335
.T87
1984

11158924

Table of Contents

AUTHOR'S PREFACE   7

ACKNOWLEDGEMENTS   9

Chapter 1   INTRODUCTION
    1.1   Non-standard logics   11
    1.2   Non-standard logics in computer science   12
    1.3   Non-standard logics in artificial intelligence   13
    1.4   Classical first-order logic   14

Chapter 2   MODALITY AND DYNAMIC LOGIC
    2.1   Modal logic   18
    2.2   A computational interpretation of modal logic   21
    2.3   A simple programming language   22
    2.4   Dynamic logic   25
    2.5   A theory of knowledge and action   28

Chapter 3   3-VALUED LOGICS AND THEIR COMPUTATIONAL
                  INTERPRETATIONS
    3.1   Introduction   32
    3.2   Three 3-valued logics   33
    3.3   Monotonicity   37
    3.4   Strictness   40

Chapter 4   **INTUITIONISTIC LOGIC: MARTIN-LÖFS THEORY**
                 OF TYPES
  4.1   Intuitionism   43
  4.2   The intuitionistic interpretation of the logical constants   45
  4.3   The language of the theory of types   48
  4.4   Judgements and rules of inference   50
  4.5   The theory of types as a programming language   53

Chapter 5   **TOWARDS A SEMANTIC THEORY OF NON-MONOTONIC**
                 INFERENCE
  5.1   Non-monotonic reasoning   59
  5.2   Non-monotonic modal theories   61
  5.3   Intuitionistic basis for non-monotonic logic   65
  5.4   Partial models and incomplete information   68
  5.5   Autoepistemic logic   73

Chapter 6   **TEMPORAL LOGIC IN ARTIFICIAL INTELLIGENCE**
  6.1   Introduction   77
  6.2   Temporal logic   79
  6.3   Two case studies   83
  6.4   Events and instants   88
  6.5   Temporal logic, specification and verification   91

Chapter 7   **FUZZY LOGIC AND EXPERT SYSTEMS**
  7.1   Fuzzification   101
  7.2   Fuzzy set theory   102
  7.3   Multi-valued logic   104
  7.4   Fuzzy logic   105
  7.5   Fuzzy logic and fuzzy set theory in expert systems   110

Chapter 8   **OTHER LOGICS AND FUTURE PROSPECTS**
  8.1   Other logics   115
  8.2   Prospects   117

INDEX   120

Author's Preface

This book is intended to serve as an elementary text and reference work on the applications of non-standard logics to artificial intelligence (AI). We have also included those applications of such logics to mainstream computer science which we believe are of some background interest to the AI specialist.

Chapters 2 and 4 are largely concerned with computer science in general but, in particular, with the problem of program specification and verification. Chapters 3, 5, 6, and 7 deal with specific applications of non-standard logics to various areas of AI. Chapter 3 also provides some background material for the topics of the following chapters. Apart from some preliminary discussion of the predicate calculus in Chapter 1, each of the chapters is very largely self-contained. We have, therefore, tried to cater for the reader who might only be concerned with a selection of the topics covered in the book. Each chapter contains a reasonably extensive bibliography together with suggestions for further reading.

Although many of the chapters are concerned with specific applications of the various logics to computer science and AI, each of the chapters contains a quite elementary and self-contained introduction to one area of non-standard logic.

Raymond Turner
Dept of Computer Science,
University of Essex,
Wivenhoe Park,
Colchester, Essex.

Acknowledgements

I would like to thank Martin Henson, Jim Doran, Libor Spacek, Sam Steel, and Pat Hayes for many insightful comments and criticisms during the preparation of this text. A special thank you also to Marisa Bostock for typing a difficult text with speed, efficiency, and just a few complaints.

1

Introduction

1.1 NON-STANDARD LOGICS

The term 'non-standard logic' is a generic term which has been used to refer to any logic other than the classical propositional or predicate calculus. Roughly, such logics can be divided into two groups: those that rival classical logics and those which extend it. In the first group we place the multi-valued logics, fuzzy logic and intuitionistic logic, while the second is to encompass modal and temporal logics. We shall not try to make this distinction precise but rather attempt to illustrate the division by reference to the various logics cited.

Rival systems of logic do not differ from classical propostional or predicate logic in terms of the language employed. Rather, rival logics differ in that certain of the theorems of classical logic are rendered false in the non-standard systems. Perhaps the most notorious example of this concerns the law of excluded middle, A or not A. This is provable in classical logic but not in either intuitionisitic logic or in any of the standard systems of 3-valued logic.

Logics which extend classical logic sanction all the theorems of classical logic but, generally, supplement it in two ways. Firstly, the languages of these non-standard logics are extensions of those of classical logic, and secondly, the theorems of these non-standard systems supplement those of classical logic. Usually, such supplementation is provided by the enriched vocabulary of these non-standard systems. For example, modal logic is enriched by the addition of two new operators L (it is necessary that) and M (it is possible that). Under this new regime the sentence $A \rightarrow MA$ is taken as axiomatic. The addition of such axioms, and appropriate rules of inference involving these operators, facilitates the derivation of theorems which are not even expressible in the language of the predicate calculus.

This division is not watertight, but then it is not meant to be; it is only meant to provide a rough guide through the labyrinth of non-standard logics. For a more detailed discussion of this classification the reader should consult Haack (1974).

Our primary interest concerns the application of these logics to artificial intelligence, although we shall review some of the applications made of such logics to mainstream computer science where we consider such applications to be of some interest to AI itself. As a consequence, in our expositions of these various logics, a great many details will be glossed over or even omitted and, in general, we shall discuss only those aspects of the subject which pertain to our intended domains of application. Nevertheless, in the process we shall provide a reasonably self-contained introduction to the more common members of the genre of non-strandard logics.

1.2 NON-STANDARD LOGICS IN COMPUTER SCIENCE

In recent years non-standard logics have been imported into a great many areas of computer science and, in particular, into those aspects of the subject which pertain to the specification and verification of programs.

Modal logic, for example, has been employed in the form of dynamic logic (Harel 1979) to facilitate the statement and proof of properties of programs. Programs are viewed as relations between states and, consequently, each program implicitly induces a modal operator. This enables one to express, in a rather natural way, properties of programs such as partial correctness.

Temporal logic has found application, in the work of Manna & Pnueli (1979), to the specification and verification of concurrent programs. They introduce a form of temporal logic as a way of reasoning about sequences of states induced by such programs. Halpern, Manna, & Maszkowski (1983) have employed certain variations on temporal logic to specify hardware circuits.

Intuitionistic logic, in the form of Martin-Löf's theory of types, provides a complete theory of the process of program specification, construction, and verification. A similar theme has been pursued by Constable (1971) and Beeson (1984).

The great strength of modal and temporal logics relates to their expressive power. In such systems it is possible to express properties of programs in an elegant and natural way. This is in large part due to the enriched vocabulary of such logics over that of the predicate calculus. In the case of intuitionistic logic the motivation for their employment is different. We have classified intuitionistic logic as a rival to classical logic. The proponents of intuitionistic logic and mathematics claim that constructive mathematics is, generally, a more appropriate framework for computer science than classical logic and mathematics.

This book is not intended to be an exhaustive survey of the whole area. Our intention is to concentrate on those aspects which appear to have been the most influential and that offer exciting prospects for future research, especially in their application to AI itself.

1.3 NON-STANDARD LOGICS IN ARTIFICIAL INTELLIGENCE

The relevance of non-standard logics to AI has been a topic of debate since the publication of McCarthy and Hayes (1969). The history of the subject is long and controversial, and in this book we cannot hope to cover all such applications; indeed, it is not clear that such an enterprise would be at all useful. We shall concentrate on those topics which appear to have some relevance to present concerns in the subject.

Many-valued and fuzzy logics have been imported into AI to deal with areas of vagueness and incomplete information. Most expert systems, for example, are forced to take decisions when not all the facts pertaining to the decision are available. In such contexts it is natural to employ logics which, unlike classical logic, are suited to reasoning with such incomplete information. Non-monotonic logic has also been developed, largely by the AI fraternity itself, to deal with reasoning with such incomplete information. Moreover, many concepts employed in natural language and AI are claimed to be 'vague', and the necessity of reasoning with such concepts suggests that some 'logic of vagueness' is appropriate. It should be said that many of these applications are both philosophically and practically controversial, and the whole area is, at present, a hive of debate.

Modal logics, in the form of logics of knowledge, belief, and action, have been introduced into AI by Bob Moore (1984) and Kurt

Konolige (1982). Moore introduces a logic of knowledge, equivalent in power to the modal logic *S4*, and employs it in the development of a program which has the facility to reason about an agent's knowledge. Konolige employs a form of modal logic to model computer agents capable of performing cooperative tasks which involve the interaction of knowledge, action, and planning.

The introduction of temporal logic into AI is a more recent phenomenon. The main area of application has been to the formalisation of events, actions, and plans. Two papers worthy of special mention here are those of McDermott (1982) and Allen (1981).

The employment of non-standard logics in AI is not too surprising. In many respects the tasks of the philosophical logician and the AI worker are quite similar. Both are concerned with the formalisation of certain aspects of reasoning which is in every day employment. It is true that the philosophical logician has been traditionally concerned with those aspects of reasoning which are of some philosophical significance. Hence the development of logics of necessity, possibility, time, knowledge, and belief. But such issues are also of central concern to the AI worker interested in knowledge representation. Non-standard logics present the AI worker with a precise tool, which may have to be trimmed or sharpened a little, but whose strength derives from its mathematical base. Generally, such logics have a well-defined and clean semantic theory and potentially offer the AI worker a tool of great precision and elegance.

1.4 CLASSICAL FIRST-ORDER LOGIC

Our discussion of non-standard logics will be built upon a foundation of classical first-order logic. It seems prudent, therefore, to provide a brief exposition of first-order logic. Much of the notation that we shall employ here will be used throughout the book.

The syntax of first-order logic deploys a set of individual variables $x_0, \ldots, x_n, \ldots$ together with a set R_n (for each $n > 0$) of n-place relation symbols and a set f_n of n-place function symbols (for each $n \geqslant 0$). We shall later use *Var* for the set of variables and *Fun* for the set of function symbols. In addition, the basic symbols of the language L include the logical connectives &, v, ~, →, ↔, the quantifiers ∀ and ∃, and equality. Well-formed formulae (wff) are constructed from certain atomic wff by means of the logical connectives and quantifiers. The atomic wff are of the form $C(t_0, \ldots, t_{n-1})$ where C is an n-place relation symbol (equality (=) is two-place) and each t_i is a term where t is a term if either it is an individual variable or it is of the form $f(t'_0, \ldots, t'_{m-1})$ where the t'_i are terms and f is an m-place function symbol (in particular, the zero place function symbols are terms). More complex wff are formed by conjuction (&), disjunction (∨), negation (~), and quantification in the following way: if A and B are already wff then so are $A \& B$, $A \vee B$, $\sim A$, $A \rightarrow B$, $A \leftrightarrow B$, $\forall x A$, $\exists x A$. Where there is no danger of confusion we shall drop the subscripts and superscripts on the constants and variables.

Classical first-order logic is defined by specifying a finite set of axiom schemata and rules of inference. There are many different ways in which it is presented in the literature, but the following presentation is perhaps the most common.

Axioms

For any wffs A, B, C of L

(1) $A \rightarrow (B \rightarrow A)$

(2) $(A \rightarrow (B \rightarrow C)) \rightarrow ((A \rightarrow B) \rightarrow (A \rightarrow C))$

(3) $(\sim B \rightarrow \sim A) \rightarrow ((\sim B \rightarrow A) \rightarrow B)$

(4) $\forall x A(x) \rightarrow A(t)$ where t is a term free of x in $A(x)$, that is, no unbound occurrences of x in A lie within the scope of any quantifier $(\forall x')$ where x' is a variable in t.

(5) $(\forall x)(A \rightarrow B) \rightarrow (A \rightarrow \forall x B)$ where A contains no free occurrences of x.

Rules of inference

MP $\dfrac{A \qquad\qquad A \rightarrow B}{B}$

GEN $\dfrac{A}{\forall x A}$

A *proof* is any sequence of the form $A_1, \ldots, A_n$ where each A_i is either an instance of an axiom schemata or follows from earlier members of the sequence by an application of MP or GEN. A *theorem* is any wff which results from a proof, that is, the last member of such a sequence.

The semantics for the predicate calculus is furnished by the following notion.

Definition 4.1 A *first-order frame M* consists of a non-empty domain D, together with a function which assigns to each n-place function symbol f a function f' from $D^n \rightarrow D$ and to each n-place relation constant, C, an element C' of 2^{D^n}.

In order to provide the semantics for L with respect to such a frame, we shall employ an assignment function g which assigns to each individual variable an element of D. We employ the notation

$$M \vDash_g A$$

to indicate that the assignment function g *satisfies* the wff A in the frame M.

(1) $M \vDash_g C(t_0, \ldots, t_{n-1})$ iff $\langle Val(t_0, g), \ldots, Val(t_{n-1}, g)\rangle \in C'$.
   where
   $Val(t, g) = g(t)$, if t is an individual variable
   and $f'(Val(t'_0, g), \ldots, Val(t'_{m-1}, g))$ if t
   is of the form $f(t'_0, \ldots, t'_{m-1})$.

(2) $M \vDash_g \sim A$ iff $M \nvDash_g A$

(3) $M \vDash_g A \& B$ iff $M \vDash_g A$ and $M \vDash_g B$

(4) $M \vDash_g \forall x A$ iff $M \vDash_{g(d|x)} A$ for each d in D
   where $g(d|x)$ is that assignment function identical to g except on the variable x; here it assigns the value d.

The truth-conditions for the other connectives can be deduced from the equivalences

$$
\begin{array}{lcl}
A \vee B & \leftrightarrow & \sim(\sim A\ \&\ \sim B) \\
A \rightarrow B & \leftrightarrow & \sim A \vee B \\
A \leftrightarrow B & \leftrightarrow & (A \rightarrow B)\ \&\ (B \rightarrow A) \\
\exists x A & \leftrightarrow & \sim \forall x \sim A.
\end{array}
$$

Definition 4.2 A wff A is *universally valid* iff for each frame M and each assignment function g, $M \vDash_g A$.

These two notions (that is, being a theorem and being universally valid) are connected by the completeness theorem.

Theorem 4.3 (Completeness) A wff of the predicate calculus is a theorem iff it is universally valid.

This completes our review of classical logic. The reader will not be required to know anything else about classical logic other than that explicitly mentioned. For more details the reader should consult Mendelson (1964).

BIBLIOGRAPHICAL NOTES

The book of Susan Haack (Haack 1974) is a good starting point for the student of non-standard logic especially in regard to the philosphical foundations of the subject. This book contains a non-technical introduction to most areas of non-standard logic. The paper by McCarthy & Hayes (1969) was one of the first papers to advocate the use of such logics in AI and is still worth reading in order to gain some general perspective on the subject.

Allen, J. F. (1981) 'An interval based representation of temporal knowledge' in: *Proc. 7th Int. Joint Conf. on Artificial Intelligence 1981* 221–226.

Beeson (1984) 'Proving programs and programming proofs' in: *Proc. 7th Int. Congress of Logic, Methodology and Philosophy of Science, Salzburg, 1983.* Forthcoming in *Logic, methodology and the philosphy of science VIII,* North Holland Studies in Logic.

Constable, R. L. (1971) 'Constructive mathematics and automatic program writers' in: *Proc. IFIP Conf. 1971,* North Holland.

Haack, S. (1974) *Deviant logic,* Cambridge University Press.

Halpern, J. Manna, Z., & Moszwkowski, B. (1983) 'A hardware semantics based upon temporal intervals', in: *Proc. 19th Colloqium on Automata, Languages and Programming.* Springer Lecture Notes in Computer Science, Vol. 154, 278–292.

Harel, D. (1979) *First order dynamic logic,* Springer Verlag, Lecture Notes in Computer Science, Vol 68.

Konolige, K. (1982) 'A first-order formalisation of knowledge and action for a multi-agent planning system' in: *Machine Intelligence 10,* ed. Hayes, J. E., Michie, D., & Pao, Y-H., Ellis Horwood, 41–72.

Manna, Z. & Pneuli, A. (1979) 'The modal logic of programs', *Proc. 6th Int. Colloquium on Automata, Languages and Programming,* Lecture Notes in Computer Science, Vol. 71, Springer Verlag, 385–411.

McCarthy, J. & Hayes, P. (1969) 'Some Philosophical problems from the standpoint of artificial intelligence' in: *Machine Intelligence 4,* ed. Meltzer & Michie, D. Edinburgh University Press.

McDermott, (1982) 'A temporal logic for reasoning about actions and plans', *Cognitive Science* 6 101–155.

Mendelson, E. (1964) *An introduction to mathematical logic,* Van Nostrand, Reinhold, Princetown, New Jersey.

Moore, R. C. (1984) 'A formal theory of knowledge and action', in: *Formal theories of the common sense world,* ed. Hobbs, J. R. & R. C. Moore, Ablex Pub. Co.

2

Modality and dynamic logic

2.1 MODAL LOGIC

Modal logic is concerned with arguments involving the concepts of necessity and possibility. A necessary truth is one which could not be otherwise; a contingent truth is one which could. The distinction is often explained by reference to the notion of 'possible world': a necessary truth is true in all possible worlds, whereas a contingent truth is true in the actual world but not in all possible worlds. Such an account is, of course, not entirely adequate since the notion of 'possible world' is not a completely clear one. By way of further explanation of this notation we can do no better than cite an illustration due to Bradley & Swartz (1979).

> The year is A.D. 4272. Lazarus Long is 2360 years old. Although he has been near death many times, he hasn't — unlike his biblical namesake — required the intervention of a miracle to recover. He simply checks himself (or is taken by force) into a Rejuvenation Clinic from time to time. When we last hear of him he is undergoing rejuvenation again. The year is 4291 and Lazarus is being treated in his own portable clinic aboard the star-yacht 'Dora' after travelling back in time to his birthplace in Kansas and being 'mortally wounded' in the trenches 'somewhere in France'.

This is but part of what happens to the Lazarus Long of Robert A. Heinlein's novel *Time enough for love*. In this novel the author builds upon a framework of persons and events that actually occurred, and leads us to a fantasy world different from the actual one. Such a world is a candidate for the qualification 'possible world'. Now it is, of course, not at all clear that the events which happened to Lazarus Long are in any sense possible. We might doubt, for example, that time travel is possible. But, whatever decisions we take over such individual cases, it seems clear that some things are possible and some things are not; some supposed worlds are possible and certain others are not.

The distinction between necessary and contingent truths is a metaphysical one and should not be confused with the distinction between *a priori* and *a posteriori* truths. An *a priori* truth is one which can be *known* independently of experience, and an *a posteriori* truth is one which cannot. Such notions appeal to epistemic considerations. It is not feasible in a text such as this to give an adequate account of any of these issues. The whole area bristles with philosophical difficulties. Instead, we shall concentrate on the formal aspects of the subject and its possible application to computer science.

In this section we shall be concerned with first-order modal logic and its semantic interpretation. The language of first-order modal logic, L_{ML}, is obtained from that of the predicate calculus (L) by the addition of two new operators: L (to be read 'it is necessary that') and M (to be read 'it is possible that'). More precisely, L_{ML} is obtained from L by the addition of the following clause: If A is a wff of L_{ML} then so are LA and MA.

Unlike the classical connectives $\sim$, &, v, $\rightarrow$ etc., these operators do not admit of a truth-functional interpretation. Instead, their interpretation enlists the notion of a possible world. Roughly, MA is true if A is true in some possible world, and LA is true if A is true in every possible world. To make these matters formally more precise, we need to introduce the notion of a 'modal frame'.

Definition 1.1 A *modal frame M* is a structure $\langle W, D, R, F \rangle$ where

(i) W is a non-empty set (of 'possible worlds');

(ii) D is a non-empty domain of 'individuals';

(iii) R is a binary relation of 'accessibility' on W;

(iv) F is a function which assigns to each pair consisting of a function symbol (n-place, $n \geqslant 0$) and an element w of W, a function from D^n to D, and to each pair consisting of a (n-place, $n > 0$) relation symbol and an element w of W, an element of 2^{D^n}.

The function F should be thought of as assigning to each function symbol f and world w the extension of the function named by f in w, and similarly for relation symbols. The point is that certain predicates, for example, might be true of different objects in different possible worlds. A more general notion of frame would insist that the domain of individuals should also vary from world to world. We have not chosen this course, simply because the application that we have in mind does not require it. The accessibility relation is meant to capture the intuition that, from the perspective of a certain world w, certain other worlds might be deemed possible, which would not be taken as so, from the perspective of a world different to w. The notion of what is possible and what is not is taken to be a relative one; what is possible depends on how things happen to be.

The interpretation of L_{ML} in such a modal frame differs from the interpretation of the predicate calculus in that the domain W plays a crucial role. The interpretation, however, is still given relative to an assignment function g which assigns elements of D to the individual variables. (For convenience we shall write wRw' to indicate that $\langle w, w' \rangle$ satisfies the relation R.) We shall employ the notation

$$M \vDash_{g, w} A$$

to indicate that g *satisfies* the wff A, at the world w, in the frame M. This is defined recursively as follows.

(1) $M \vDash_{w, g} C(t_0, \ldots, t_{n-1})$ iff $\langle Val(t_0, w, g), \ldots, Val(t_{n-1}, w, g) \rangle \in F(w, C)$

where $Val(t, w, g) = \begin{cases} g(t) & \text{if } t \text{ is a variable} \\ F(w, f)(Val(t'_0, w, g), \ldots, Val(t'_{m-1}, w, g)) \\ \qquad \text{if } t = f(t'_0, \ldots, t'_{m-1}) \end{cases}$

(2) $M \vDash_{w, g} t_1 = t_2$ iff $Val(t_1, w, g) = Val(t_2, w, g)$

(3) $M \vDash_{w, g} A \& B$ iff $M \vDash_{w, g} A$ and $M \vDash_{w, g} B$

(4) $M \vDash_{w, g} {\sim} A$ iff $M \nvDash_{w, g} A$

(5) $M \vDash_{w, g} \forall x A$ iff   for each d in D, $M \vDash_{w, g(d \mid x)} A$

(6) $M \vDash_{w, g} MA$ iff   there exists a $w' \in W$ such that wRw' and $M \vDash_{w', g} A$.

The interpretation of the other logical connectives is given by definition in the standard way. In addition we define $LA =_{df} {\sim}M{\sim}A$.

The formal properties of R determine the modal logic (axioms and rules of inference) which are deemed to be valid. We shall say that a wff is *valid* with respect to a particular class of frames C iff it is satisfied by each assignment function and possible world, in each frame in C. So, for example, if we take C to be all those frames where R is just reflexive, then we obtain the logic commonly known as *T*. If in addition, we insist that R be transitive we obtain *S4*, whereas the modal logic *S5* is obtained by insisting that R is reflexive, transitive and symmetrical (that is, an equivalence relation). The modal logic *T* is characterised by the axiom schemata of the Predicate Calculus plus the following axiom schemata:

$$LA \rightarrow A$$
$$L(A \rightarrow B) \rightarrow (LA \rightarrow LB)$$

and rule of inference:

$$\frac{A}{LA}$$

referred to as necessitation. *S4* is obtained by the addition of

$$LA \rightarrow LLA$$

to *T*; and *S5* by the addition of

$$MA \rightarrow LMA$$

to *S4*. Since we have employed frames where the domain of individuals remains fixed, the Barcan formula

$$\forall x (LA) \rightarrow L (\forall x \, A)$$

is true in all our frames.

2.2 A COMPUTATIONAL INTERPRETATION OF MODAL LOGIC

The classical interpretation of the modalities, in terms of the metaphysical concepts of necessity and possibility, has very little to do with the more mundane world of computer science. The latter derives its inspiration from contemplating notions like 'program', 'algorithm', and 'computation'. It is surprising, therefore, that modal logic admits of an interpretation in which these notions play a central role. The idea behind the interpretation is simple enough and derives its impetus from a perspective on the semantics of programming languages which views the meaning of programs as somehow derivative of their impact on the store of some abstract machine. More explicitly, consider a simple assignment statement '$x := 4$'. It is natural to view the meaning of this statement as a function which, given the store of some appropriate abstract machine, updates the store by binding the value 4 to the variable x. In general, each such statement, in a deterministic programming language, can be viewed as such a function. This is the view taken, for example, in the denotational semantics of programming languages. This perspective naturally generalises to the non-deterministic case, where a statement is now viewed not as a function on the store of the machine, but rather as a binary relation on such.

Under this interpretation each such statment G, in a programming language, induces 'modal' operators M_G and L_G. Moreover, under such a perspective, the role of 'possible worlds' is now taken over by 'stores' of the underlying machine, and $M_G A$ will be true, in a store or state s, just in case there is a terminating state s', reachable from s via G, in which A is true. It is this interpretation of the modalities that we shall now explore.

2.3 A SIMPLE PROGRAMMING LANGUAGE

To scrutinise this interpretation of the modal operators more carefully we here present the syntax and semantics of a simple (non-deterministic) programming language $-$ NL. In the next section we shall study a modal logic based upon this language.

As regards the syntax of NL we introduce three classes of constructs: *Exp, Bexp,* and *Stat. Exp* is the class of expressions whose elements will be denoted by $e_0, e_1, e_2, \ldots$; *Bexp* is the class of Boolean expressions with typical elements $b_0, b_1, b_2, \ldots$, and *Stat* is the class of statements with typical elements $G_0, G_1, G_2, G_3, \ldots$.

We shall, in addition, enlist the domains *Fun,* of function symbols, and *Var,* of variables, introduced in the first chapter.

The classes *Exp* and *Stat* are specified by the following BNF definition:

$$e ::= x \mid f^n(e_1, \ldots, e_n)$$
$$G ::= x := e \mid b? \mid G_1; G_2 \mid G_1 \cup G_2 \mid \text{Loop } G$$

The class *Bexp* will remain, for the moment, unspecified. Intuitively, $x := e$ is a simple assignment statement which attaches the value of e to the variable x. The statement $b?$ tests for the truth of the Boolean expression b, and $G_1; G_2$ represents the sequencing of statements. The statement $G_1 \cup G_2$ means 'do G_1 or G_2, the choice being non-deterministic', and Loop G means 'do G any (non-negative) number of times, the choice being non-deterministic'.

To provide a more precise semantics for this language we need to describe the semantic domains or sets required for its specification.

We shall assume, to begin with, that we are provided with what we shall call an *NL — model structure:*

$$N = \langle D, F \rangle,$$

where D is a non-empty domain of values and F is a function which assigns to each n-place function symbol a function from D^n to D, and to each n-place relation symbol an element of 2^{D^n} (we shall not explicitly exploit this interpretation of relation symbols until the next section).

To capture the full import of the assignment statement we require some way of keeping track of the values attached to variables. To this end, we introduce a domain of Stores (*Sto*) with typical element s. This domain consists of all functions from *Var* to D:

$$s \in Sto = (Var \to D).$$

Expressions, relative to such a store, get assigned their values in D. This is achieved by, recursively, defining a semantic function

$$E : Exp \to [Sto \to D]$$

as follows:

(E1) $E\,[x]_s^N = s\,(x)$

(E2) $E\,[f(e_1, \ldots, e_n)]_s^N = F(f)\,(E\,[e_1]_s^N, \ldots, E\,[e_n]_s^N)$

This is exactly the interpretation given to terms in the predicate calculus where assignment functions play the role of the store. Because of the more syntactically complex regime of programming languages we have made things a little more palatable by being somewhat more explicit.

Statements are to be interpreted as sets of ordered pairs of stores; a pair of stores $\langle s_1, s_2 \rangle$ will be in the set denoted by G, if s_2 is a possible final store or state for G given the initial state s_1. The relational interpretation of statements is, of course, an artifact of the non-determinisitic nature of our language. Given these intuitions, the semantic function for statements must have the following form:

$$S : Stat \to 2^{Sto \times Sto}.$$

Once agin, this is specified recursively, where the recursion follows the BNF definition of statements.

Firstly, however, we need to define a couple of operations on the domain $2^{Sto \times Sto}$. Let P, Q be elements of $2^{Sto \times Sto}$, then define

$$P \circ Q = \{\langle s_1, s_2 \rangle : \exists s_3 \in Sto \text{ such that}$$
$$\langle s_1, s_3 \rangle \in Q \text{ and } \langle s_3, s_2 \rangle \in P\}$$

and $\qquad P* = \bigcup_{n \geqslant 0} P^n$

where $\qquad P^0 = \{\langle s, s \rangle : s \in Sto\}$ and $P^{n+1} = P^n \circ P$.

The first is just relation composition, and the second non-deterministically iterated composition.

We can now formally define S.

(S1) $S[x := e]^N = \{\langle s_1, s_2 \rangle : s_2 = s_1 (E[e]_{s_1}^N \mid x)\}$
where $s_1 (E[e]_{s_1}^N \mid x)$ is that store which is the function identical to s_1 except (perhaps) on the variable x; here it assigns the value $E[e]_{s_1}^N$.

(S2) $S[b?]^N = \{\langle s, s \rangle : B[b]_s^N = t\}$
We shall not specify B for the moment. We shall simply assume B assigns to each Boolean expression (relative to a store), either the value t (true) or f (false).

(S3) $S[G_1 ; G_2]^N = S[G_2]^N \circ S[G_1]^N$
The reader should observe that the relational composition reverses the chronological order of the statements: the effect of G_1 must be computed first.

(S4) $S[G_1 \cup G_2]^N = S[G_1]^N \cup S[G_2]^N$
For non-deterministic 'or' one simply computes the set-theoretic union of the possible outcomes.

(S5) $S[\text{loop } G]^N = (S[G]^N)*$
The definition of '*' captures our intuitive remarks: we are to perform G any (non-negative) number of times in a non-deterministic fashion.

The style of semantics presented for *NL* is reminiscent of that employed in denotational semantics. The main difference is that we have not insisted that any form of structure should be attached to our domains. To develop this further, however, would take us too far from our present concerns. The reader who is interested in finding out more about denotational sematics should consult Stoy (1977), Gordon (1979), or Tennent (1981).

2.4 DYNAMIC LOGIC

We now study a modal language based upon NL. The term 'Dynamic Logic' is a generic term referring to the whole class of such structures. It does not refer just to the particular modal language under scrutiny here.

Let L_{NL} be the modal language which admits the family of modal operators $\{M_G : G \in Stat\}$ and their duals $\{L_G : G \in Stat\}$.

To provide the semantics of L_{NL} we utilise a modal frame of the form

$$M = \langle Sto, D, R, F \rangle$$

where (i) $N = \langle D, F \rangle$ is an NL-model structure;
   (ii) Sto is the domain of Stores;
   (iii) $R = \{R_G : G \in Stat\}$ where
         $R_G = S[G]^N$.

Observe that the function F is independent of the store — the set of possible worlds. This is not in keeping with the standard interpretation of modal logic presented earlier, where the function and relation symbols get different interpretations in different possible worlds. The frames we consider are essentially what Harel (1979) calls 'simple'. This is, perhaps, a sufficient reason for not taking the present set-up too seriously as a plausible interpretation of modal logic. The domain Sto does not play exactly the same role formally, as 'possible worlds' do in standard interpretations of the modal operators. The emphasis here is not upon the intensional nature of functions but upon the interpretation of the modal operators themselves.

We are now in a position to provide the semantics of L_{NL}, with respect to such a modal frame.

(1) $M \vDash_s e_1 = e_2$ iff $E[e_1]_s^N = E[e_2]_s^N$

(2) $M \vDash_s C(e_0, \ldots, e_{n-1})$ iff $\langle E[e_0]_s^N, \ldots, E[e_{n-1}]_s^N \rangle \in F(C)$

(3) $M \vDash_s A \mathbin{\&} B$ iff $M \vDash_s A$ and $M \vDash_s B$

(4) $M \vDash_s \sim A$ iff $M \nvDash_s A$

(5) $M \vDash_s \forall x A$ iff for each $d \in D$, $M \vDash_{s(d\,|x)} A$

(6) $M \vDash_s M_G A$ iff there exists s' in Sto such that $sR_G s'$
                                      and $M \vDash_{s'} A$

(7) $M \vDash_s L_G A$ iff for each $s' \in Sto$, $sR_G s'$ implies
                                      $M \vDash_{s'} A$

The definition of the pure predicate calculus part of L_{NL} is the standard one where the role of the store is that traditionally taken by the assignment function. In clause (6), however, the store plays a dual role for, in addition to its role as an assignment function, it plays the role of a 'possible world': $M_G A$ is true at a store s if 'it is possible' for G to terminate in a store where A is true.

We can now complete our definition of the language NL by specifying the semantics of Boolean expressions. We shall actually permit a Boolean expression to be any *modal-free* wff of L_{NL}. In other words, we exclude the modal operators M_G (L_G) from occurring in tests of the form b? For this subset of L_{NL} we define $B[b]_s^N$ to be t just in case $M \vDash_s b$.

Given a modal frame M we follow standard procedure and say that a wff A of L_{NL} is *M-valid* iff for each $s \in Sto$, $M \vDash_s A$ and A is *valid* iff it is *M*-valid for all modal frames M.

The following are examples of valid wff:

(i) $(x = y) \rightarrow L_{G_1} M_{G_2} (x = y)$
   where
   $G_1 = \text{Loop } (x := f(f(x)))$
   $G_2 = \text{Loop } (y := f(y))$.

(ii) $L_G (x = z \lor y = u)$
   where
   $G = (x = z \, \& \, y = u)? ; (x := f(x) \cup y := f(y))$.

The first asserts that the process of repeatedly applying a function composed with itself is a special case of just repeatedly applying it; the second states that at most one of the components of the non-deterministic join is executed. More examples can be found in Harel (1979).

For details concerning axiomatisation and completeness of various first-order dynamic logics the reader should, again, consult Harel (1979).

The main virtue of such modal languages concerns their expressive power. They provide a coherent framework in which one can express many formal properties pertaining to the host programming language.

(i) *Partial correctness* of a statement G with respect to wff A and B:

$$M \vDash A \rightarrow L_G B.$$

(ii) The existence of a *terminating path* of a statement G in which a specified wff A is true:

$$M \vDash M_G A.$$

(iii) The existence of a *terminating path* of G in which A is true under the assumption B:

$$M \models B \rightarrow M_{\hat{G}} A.$$

The first example is exactly the Hoare (1969) rule of partial correctness. In that paper Hoare introduces a formalism for describing the partial correctness of programs. It was this tradition which led Pratt (1976) to the current framework. Hoare actually introduces the notation $A \{G\} B$ which means, informally, that if A holds before execution of G, and the execution of G terminates, then B holds afterwards. For example, $x = 0 \{x := x + 1\} x = 1$ states that, if $x = 0$ before execution of the assignment statement, then $x = 1$ afterwards. Under the government of dynamic logic Hoare's rule of partial correctness is thus expressed as $M \models A \rightarrow L_G B$.

To conclude we present a more concrete example of the use of dynamic logic in stating properties of programs. Consider the following program G which computes the gcd of two numbers.

$$(x \neq y?; \text{Loop} \ (x > y?; x := x - y \cup x < y?; y := y - x); x = y?)$$

In a more familiar notation the program G can be written as

> While $x \neq y$ do
>> if $x > y$ then $x := x - y$
>>> else $y := y - x$
>
> end

We are assuming here that the domain of our model is the natural numbers and $+, \cdot,$ and 0 are fixed with their ordinary meanings. The term $x - y$ stands for the difference between x and y if $x \geqslant y$, and 0 otherwise.

Now consider the following wff A

$$L_Q \ M_G \ (x = \gcd (x', y'))$$

where Q is the program statement

$$(x = x' \ \& \ y = y' \ \& \ x \cdot y > 0)?$$

Then A asserts that the program G, under the assumption that its two inputs are positive integers, terminates and computes the gcd of the inputs.

Although we have really only scratched the surface of this subject we hope we have both provided an understandable introduction to the fundamental notions of dynamic logic and have whetted the reader's appetite sufficiently to pursue the topic further. Our approach is closely based upon Harel (1979). In this text the reader will not only find extensions and variations to the language *NL* and their corresponding dynamic logics, but also a detailed metamathematical investigation of the topic including various completeness results.

2.5 A THEORY OF KNOWLEDGE AND ACTION

Although dynamic logic has, so far, found no direct application to AI, modal logic itself has. Modal logic has been utilised by AI workers where the interpretation of modal operators is furnished by attempts to build theories of belief and knowledge. The work of Moore and Konolige cited in Chapter One is of this kind. We conclude this chapter by giving a brief account of one such application.

In his thesis and in a forthcoming paper (Moore 1984) Bob Moore develops a modal logic of knowledge and action. Moore adopts the possible-world approach to the logic of knowledge introduced by Hintikka (1962). Kripke semantics for necessity and possibility can be converted into Hintikka semantics for knowledge by changing the interpretation of the accessibility relation. To analyse statements of the form KNOW (a, A) Moore, following Hintikka, introduces a relation K, such that $K(a, w_1, w_2)$ means that the possible world w_2 is compatible or consistent with that the agent a knows in the possible world w_1. In other words, for all a knows in w_1, he might just as well be in w_2. This relation of accessibility is taken to be reflexive and transitive and thus the underlying logic is *S4*.

The theory is actually stated in the metalanguage of the theory – a many-sorted first-order language which not only permits quantification over possible worlds but is also rich enough in coding machinery to represent wffs of the object language as terms. So, for example, the object language formula:

$$\text{KNOW(JOHN, } \exists x\, P(X)) \tag{1}$$

is represented in the metalanguage by the metalanguage term

$$\text{KNOW(JOHN, EXIST}(X, P(X))) \tag{2}$$

where JOHN and X are metalanguage constants and KNOW, EXIST, and P are metalanguage functions. Since (2) is a term we will want to assert its truth – or rather the truth of object language formula it denotes. This is achieved by introducing a truth-predicate TRUE into the metalanguage:

$$\text{TRUE(KNOW(JOHN, EXIST}(X, P(X)))).$$

As Moore points out, in a possible world theory of knowledge, statements about knowledge are only true relative to a possible world. To cope with this Moore introduces an axiom

$$\text{(L1) } (\forall A) (\text{TRUE}(A) \leftrightarrow T(w_0, A))$$

where $T(w, A)$ means the formula A is true in the world w and w_0 is the actual world. Other axioms govern the logical connectives, for example

$$\text{(L2) } (\forall w \ \forall AB) (T(w, \text{AND}(A, B))) \leftrightarrow (T(w, A)$$
$$\& \ T(w, B))$$

where AND is the metalanguage function representing the object language conjunction. In this way Moore is able to formalise his theory of knowledge in a first-order framework. For example

$$\text{(K1) } (\forall w_1 tA) (T(w_1, \text{KNOW}(t, A)) \leftrightarrow (\forall w_2)$$
$$(K(D(w_1, t), w_1, w_2) \to T(w_2, A)))$$

provides the possible-world analysis for object language formulas of the form $\text{KNOW}(a, A)$: $\text{KNOW}(a, A)$ is true in w_1 iff A is true in every world compatiable with what the agent, denoted by a in w_1 knows in W_2. Moore uses $D(w_1, a)$ to identify the denotation of a in w_1.

Such a formalisation of the possible-world analysis of knowledge permit inferences to be made about an agent's knowledge in a first-order framework. In the paper Moore provides a derivation of $\text{TRUE}(\text{KNOW}(a, P(C)))$ from the assumptions $\text{TRUE}(\text{KNOW}(a, P(B)))$ and $\text{TRUE}(\text{KNOW}(a, EQ(B, C)))$. This derivation uses only axiom schema such as L1, L2, and K1 together with the normal inference machinery of first-order logic.

This technique of formalising a semantic account of some intensional notion as a first-order theory seems to be a useful one in AI even if it all seems quite straightforward. At least Moore has been guided explicitly by semantic considerations, and the above manoeuvre may be seen as no more than a device for representing the theory in a way which renders it suitable for implementation as a first-order theory.

The paper is quite well-written and is certainly worthy of further consideration. The paper concludes by offering an account of action is such a framework; an account which is certainly not without merit.

BIBLIOGRAPHICAL NOTES

The best easily available introduction to dynamic logic is Harel (1979). Here the reader will find references to the vast literature of the subject. In this regard the original paper of Pratt (1976) is well worth looking at.

A rather different computational interpretation of the modalities (strictly speaking the temporal modalities) occurs in the work of Manna & Pnueli. These authors apply temporal logic to the specification and verification of concurrent programs. They introduce temporal logic as a way of reasoning about sequences of states. For more details the reader should consult section 6.5.

The book by Bradley & Swartz provides an easy introduction to the notion of possible worlds and its application to modal logic. For more technical details the reader should consult Hughes & Cresswell (1968) or Zeman (1973). The original papers of Kripke (1963, 1972) are worthy of special attention. Indeed, Kripke's paper 'Naming and necessity' is, among other things, a beautiful exposition of the foundations of modal logic.

The denotational semantics of programming languages is fully dealt with in Tennent (1981), Stoy (1977), and Gordon (1979).

Hoare (1969) has had enormous impact upon the problem of program specification and correctness and clearly inspired the original work on Dynamic logic.

Moore (1984) is one of the few insightful applications of modal logic to AI. The paper is worthy of more attention than I have given to it, and the student of AI could do worse than begin her study of the applications of non-standard logics by reading this paper.

Bradley, B. & Swartz, M. (1979) *Possible worlds,* Oxford.

Gordon, M. (1979) *The denotational description of programming languages,* Springer-Verlag.

Harel, D. (1979) *First order dynamic logic,* Springer-Verlag, Lecture Notes in Computer Science, Vol 68.

Hoare, C. A. R. (1969) 'An axiomatic basis for computer programming', *CACM* 12 576–580.

Hintikka (1962) 'Knowledge & belief', Cornell University Press, 1962.

Hughes, G. & Cresswell, M. (1968) *An introduction to modal logic,* Methuen.

Kripke, S. (1963) 'Semantical considerations on modal logic', *Acta Philosphica Fennica* **16** 83—94.

Kirpke, S. (1972) 'Naming and necessity', in *Semantics of natural language,* ed. Harman and Davidson, Reidel 253—356. Republished as *Naming & necessity,* 1980 Basil Blackwell, Oxford.

Manna, Z. & Pnueli, A. (1979) 'The modal logic of programs', *Proc. 6th Int. Colloquium on Automata, Languages and Programming,* Lecture Notes in Computer Science, Vol 71, Springer-Verlag 385—411.

Moore, R. C. (1984) 'A formal theory of knowledge and action' in: *Formal theories of the common sense world,* ed. Hobbs, J. R. and Moore, R. C. Ablex Pub. Corp. 1984.

Pratt, V. R. (1976) 'Semantical considerations on Floyd-Hoare logic', *Proc. 17th I.E.E.E. Symp. on Foundations of Computer Science.* 109—121.

Stoy, J. (1977) *Denotational semantics: the Scott-Strachey approach to programming language theory,* MIT Press.

Tennent, R. D. (1981) *Principles of programming languages,* Prentice Hall.

Zeman, J. J. (1973) *Modal logic,* Oxford.

3

3-valued logics and their computational interpretations

3.1 INTRODUCTION

Classical logic employs just two truth-values in its semantic interpretation. On the classical view any sentence is determinately either true or false. Three-valued logic, however, enlists a third truth-value which, on some interpretations at least, represents a value which is somehow intermediate between truth and falsity. There have been a host of proposals relating both to the intuitive interpretation of this third value and for the change to logic that follows in its wake. It is not our intention to survey all these various proposals, instructive as this might be. And, in any case, Susan Haack (1974, 1978) has already carried out a very thorough analysis of the spectrum of such logics.

We shall examine just three such logics, those of Kleene, Lukasiewicz, and Bochvar. We have chosen these because they are representative of the whole family of 3-valued logics. Kleene's logic, for example, is taken as the paradigm case of a logic with truth-value gaps. This must be seen in contrast to a logic which admits more than two genuine truth-values. We begin by examining these three logics, paying some attention to the actual intuitions which led to their creation. Later we shall examine the computational tractability of these logics. In this regard we shall be largely concerned with the feasibility of such logics as logics which govern the behaviour of a certain class of programs whose intent is to garner knowledge about their environments in a systematic way.

3.2 THREE 3-VALUED LOGICS

Kleene's logic was originally conceived to accommodate undecided mathematical statements. The third truth-value, intuitively, represents 'undecided' (u) and, as such, its assignment to a wff is not intended to indicate that the wff is neither true nor false. Rather, its purpose is to signal a state of partial ignorance. Indeed, enshrined in Kleene's logic is the principle that where one can determine the truth-value (true or false) of a compound wff from its components, the wff should be assigned that truth-value, regardless of whether or not certain of its components are undecided. So, for example, A & B will be assigned the value t if both A and B are assigned the value t, and it will be assigned the value f if one of A or B is assigned the value f (this will be so even if u is assigned to the other).

Before we proceed to provide Kleene's truth-tables in full, it is worth pointing out that Kleene also introduced a set of weak-connectives which assign the undecided value to any wff which has at least one undecided component. The weak interpretation actually corresponds to that of Bochvar which we shall examine shortly.

Kleene's strong 3-valued connectives

$\neg A$	
t	f
f	t
u	u

$A \wedge B$	t	f	u
t	t	f	u
f	f	f	f
u	u	f	u

$A \vee B$	t	f	u
t	t	t	t
f	t	f	u
u	t	u	u

$A \rightarrow B$	t	f	u
t	t	f	u
f	t	t	t
u	t	u	u

$A \leftrightarrow B$	t	f	u
t	t	f	u
f	f	t	u
u	u	u	u

Viewing universal and existential quantification as infinite conjunction and disjunction respectively, we can, in the same spirit, introduce the following operators:

$$\bigwedge_{i \in I} d_i = \begin{cases} t & \text{if each } d_i = t \\ f & \text{if some } d_i = f \\ u & \text{otherwise;} \end{cases} \qquad \bigvee_{i \in I} d_i = \begin{cases} t & \text{if some } d_i = t \\ f & \text{if each } d_i = f \\ u & \text{otherwise.} \end{cases}$$

One of the clearest interpretations of Kleene's logic employs some form of epistemological metaphor. An assertion p is assigned the value u just in case it is not *known* to be either true or false. For example, imagine a detective trying to solve a murder. He may conjecture that Jones the Baker killed the victim. He cannot, at present, assign a truth-value to his conjecture, but it is certainly either true or false.

Luckasiewicz developed his logic to deal with future contingent statements. The only formal difference between his connectives and those of Kleene relates to the conditional and biconditional.

$A \rightarrow B$	t	f	i		$A \leftrightarrow B$	t	f	i
t	t	f	i		t	t	f	i
f	t	t	t		f	f	t	i
i	t	i	t		i	i	i	t

Observe that under Lukasiewicz's interpretation the conditional is assigned the value true when both the antecedent and consequent are indeterminate (i). Consequently, his system, unlike Kleene's, preserves the law of identity.

As we have said, Lukasiewicz's logic was inspired by considerations relating to contingent statements about the future. According to him, such statements are not just neither true nor false but are indeterminate in some metaphysical sense. It is not only that we do not know their truth-value but rather that they do not possess one. Intuitively, then, the interpretation of i differs from that of u: an assignment of u represents a truth-value gap whereas an assignment of i signifies that the statement cannot be assigned the value true or false; it is not simply that we do not have sufficient information available to decide the truth value but rather the statement does not have one.

Lukasiewicz motivates his 3-valued logic by means of an argument which ultimately stems from Aristotle. The conclusion of the argument is a fatal one: if one assumes that statements about the future are *now* either true or false one is committed to fatalism.

Both Lukasiewicz's interpretation of Aristotle and the validity of his argument are disputed. Indeed, his argument seems to rest upon an equivocation between sentences of the form $L(A \rightarrow B)$ and $LA \rightarrow LB$. Whatever the merits of his argument, however, it may still turn out that his logic has some other applications. Reichenbach (1944), for example, has argued for the adoption of a 3-valued logic (which is an extension of Lukasiewicz's with more operators) in order to solve certain problems in quantum mechanics. We shall shortly look at the possibility of computationally motivated interpretations.

Bochvar's 3-valued logic was directly inspired by considerations relating to the semantic paradoxes. Consider the sentence 'this sentence is false'. If it is true then it must be false; if it is false then it must be true. There have been many proposals relating to how one might deal with such sentences ranging from Russell's ramified theory of types and Tarski's hierarchy of truth predicates, to the more recent contributions of Kripke and Gupta. Bochvar's proposal adopts a strategy which heralds a change of logic. According to Bochvar, such sentences are neither true nor false but rather 'paradoxical' or 'meaningless'. This leads to the following matrices (where m signifies an attachment of meaninglessness):

Bochvar's connectives

$\neg A$	
t	f
f	t
m	m

$A \wedge B$	t	f	m
t	t	f	m
f	f	f	m
m	m	m	m

$A \vee B$	t	f	m
t	t	t	m
f	t	f	m
m	m	m	m

$A \rightarrow B$	t	f	m
t	t	f	m
f	t	t	m
m	m	m	m

In the case of universal and existential quantification we can, in the spirit of Bochvar, define operators:

$$\bigwedge_{i \in I} d_i = \begin{cases} t & \text{if each } d_i = t \\ f & \text{if each } d_i \neq m \text{ and some } d_i = f \\ m & \text{otherwise} \end{cases}$$

$$\bigvee_{i \in I} d_i = \begin{cases} t & \text{if each } d_i \neq m \text{ and some } d_i = t \\ f & \text{if each } d_i = f \\ m & \text{otherwise.} \end{cases}$$

These conform to the principle that m is in some sense 'infectious': if one component is assigned the value m then the whole is assigned the value m.

Bochvar also adds an 'assertion operator' which, following Haack (1978), I shall write as 'T'. It is given by the following matrix.

$$
\begin{array}{c|c}
A & TA \\
\hline
t & t \\
f & f \\
m & f
\end{array}
$$

This facilitates the definition of 'external' connectives:

$$
\begin{aligned}
\neg A &= \neg\, TA \\
A \wedge B &= TA \wedge TB \\
A \vee B &= TA \vee TB \\
A \rightarrow B &= TA \rightarrow TB
\end{aligned}
$$

The matrices for the external connectives always have t or f as output, and the classical 2-valued tautologies are precisely the wffs which take the value t regardless of the assignments to their components.

Whatever the worth of Bochvar's proposal regarding the paradoxes, the logic itself may prove to admit of plausible computational interpretations. We shall examine this possibility shortly.

We are now in a position to consider the semantics of the predicate calculus within the administration of 3-valued logic. A 3-valued semantics will differ from classical semantics in the form of the models employed. Such models enlist the notion of partial predicates where a *partial (k-ary) predicate, r* on E $(k \geqslant 1)$, is meant a partial function r from E^k to $\{t, f\}$. With the aid of the symbol 'u' every such predicate can be identified with a function $r\colon E^k \rightarrow \{t, f, u\}$, and we shall actually employ this latter representation.

Definition 2.1 A *partial model* for L is a structure $M = \langle D, F \rangle$ where D is a non-empty set and F is a function which assigns to each n-place relation symbol C $(n > 0)$ of L an n-place function C^M from D^n to $\{t, f, u\}$.

The interpretation of L, in such a model, is much the same as in the classical analysis, but here we utilise some form of 3-valued connectives. We shall illustrate the semantics by reference to Kleene's connectives, but any of the three families we have considered could be employed. For convenience, we shall assume that each element d of D is named by some individual constant d'. This will somewhat enhance the readability of what follows. In particular, we make no reference to assignment functions in the following definition. We shall also assume, for pedagogical reasons, that our language admits of no n-place function symbols for $n > 0$. We provide semantics by associating with each closed wff (sentence) of L a truth-value as follows:

Kleene semantics for L

$$
\begin{aligned}
(1)\quad & [C(d'_0, \ldots, d'_{n-1})]^M & = & \quad C^M(d_0, \ldots, d_{n-1}) \\
(2)\quad & [{\sim}A]^M & = & \quad \neg[A]^M \\
(3)\quad & [A \,\&\, B]^M & = & \quad [A]^M \wedge [B]^M \\
(4)\quad & [A \to B]^M & = & \quad [A]^M \to [B]^M \\
(5)\quad & [A \vee B]^M & = & \quad [A]^M \vee [B]^M \\
(6)\quad & [\forall x\, A(x)]^M & = & \quad \bigwedge_{d \in D} [A(d)]^M \\
(7)\quad & [\exists x\, A(x)]^M & = & \quad \bigvee_{d \in D} [A(d)]^M
\end{aligned}
$$

where for illustrative purposes the connectives $\neg, \vee, \to, \wedge, \bigwedge, \bigvee$ are Kleene's strong connectives. To obtain the other logics we have only to make the appropriate changes to the above logical connectives. For example, in the case of Lukasiewicz one would only need to change the interpretation of implication, but in the case of Bochvar the interpretation of all the connectives save negative would have to be changed.

3.3 MONOTONICITY

Imagine a robot whose objective is to prod and probe its environment in an effort to garner knowledge. We are to suppose that it is equipped with visual and tactile systems which enable it to abstract information from the environment. At any given point in our robot's endeavour it will have gleaned certain knowledge: it will know that certain things are true and certain other are false. But its knowledge will, in general, be incomplete. As time proceeds, however, the robot will increase its stock of truths. We are thus assuming that the robot never discards information or revises its beliefs. The robot is to be seen as nothing more than a fact-collecting device which only notes which objects stand in which relation to each other.

Implicit, then, in our description of the robot are two assumptions:

(I) The robot will, in general, be in a state of partial ignorance;
(II) The robot never discards or revises its beliefs.

What logic(s) is appropriate to describe the activity of such a robot? Assumption (I) suggests that some form of 3-valued logic is necessary. We require a logic which is geared to deal with incomplete information. The second assumption further constrains the class of appropriate logics. Assertions once deemed true (or false) must remain so; after all, new information never causes our robot to revise its beliefs. This means that appropriate logics must possess a certain property of 'monotonicity'.

To explore these assumptions more carefully we need to decide upon a way of representing the robots model of the world. In the present context it seems quite natural to use our notion of a partial model. Such a model encodes information about the objects in the robot's environment in terms of the relations which hold between them.

As our robot moves from one state of knowledge to another, collecting facts about its environment, its internal model changes in that more objects in the environment are observed to satisfy the relations. We can phrase this phenomenon in terms of the following ideas.

Consider the set of truth-values $\{t, f, u\}$ (or $\{t, f, i\}$, $\{t, f, m\}$). This set possesses a natural partial ordering $\geqslant$ defined by: $t \geqslant u$, $f \geqslant u$, $t \geqslant f$, and $f \geqslant t$ etc. Pictorially, we can represent this as follows:

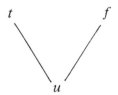

Definition 3.1 Let M and M' be partial models of L with common domain D. We shall say that M' is an *extension* of M (written $M \leqslant M'$) iff for each n-place $(n > 0)$ relation constant C of L, $C^M \leqslant C^{M'}$ in the sense that for each $e_0, \ldots, e_{n-1}$ in D, $C^M (e_0, \ldots, e_{n-1}) \leqslant C^{M'} (e_0, \ldots, e_{n-1})$.

Assumption (II) now has a rather interesting consequence. Suppose that G is the procedure which represents our robot's behaviour, so that formally G can be represented as a function which sends partial models to partial models — it abstracts information from the environment and modifies the robot's data base accordingly. Assumption (II) can now be made explicit: the function G is monotonic, that is, $M \leqslant M'$ implies $G(M) \leqslant G(M')$. Under this assumption G possesses a 'minimal fixed point'.

Theorem 3.2 (Fixed Point Theorem) Let G be a monotonic operator on partial models of L. For any partial model M such that $M \leqslant G(M)$ there exists a least M^* with $M \leqslant M^*$ and $G(M^*) = M^*$.

Proof (By transfinite induction.) For simplicity, we assume our models have the form $M = \langle D, R \rangle$ where R is an n-place relation. The following proof easily extends to the more general case.

Define R^α, for ordinals α, by $R^0 = R$, $R^{\alpha+1} = G(R^\alpha)$ and $R^\lambda = \cup R^\alpha$ for limit ordinal λ. It is easy to prove, by induction on $\alpha < \lambda$

α, that $R^\alpha \leqslant R^{\alpha+1}$. It follows that $\alpha < \beta$ implies $R^\alpha \leqslant R^\beta$. It follows that there exists a *least* α^* with $R^{\alpha^*} = G(R^{\alpha^*})$. Let this be R^* and $M^* = \langle D, R^* \rangle$. Now suppose $R \leqslant R'$ and $R' = G(R')$. Then, once again, it is easy to prove by induction on α that $R^* \leqslant R'$. So R^* is the minimal fixed point of G.

The fixed point represents all the information that may be garnered by means of G. There may still be things in the environment that may remain undecided. The fixed point only represents the total information that can be obtained by the procedure G.

Suppose that we now assume that our robot, although just a fact-collector, does have access to the language of the predicate calculus and to its semantic function. We are to imagine, therefore, that it is able to evaluate sentences of L from the perspective of its internal model. This, of course, is only realistic, from a computational perspective, if the partial model has a finite domain. It is worth noting, however, that this assumption is not necessary to derive any of the formal results which follow.

Suppose further that we are able to interrogate the robot in order to discover the status of any sentence A of L. If the robot is behaving in a way compatible with assumption (II), then we should expect that any future request, concerning the status of A, should be consistent with that already obtained. For example, if $[A]^M = t$ then $[A]^{M'} = t$, for each $M' \geqslant M$. Any logic appropriate to describe the activity of our robot must, therefore, meet this requirement. Certain 3-valued logics obey this constraint, but certain others do not. We shall shortly examine each of our logics to see which satisfy this requirement, but first we require some preliminary ideas. Let F be a function $\{t, f, u\}^I \rightarrow \{t, f, u\}$ where I is some index set. Then we shall say that F is *monotonic* iff for each d, d' in $\{t, f, u\}^I$, if $d_i \leqslant d'_i$, for each $i \in I$, then $F(d) \leqslant F(d')$.

Each of the Kleene connectives $\neg, \vee, \wedge, \rightarrow, \bigwedge, \bigvee$ is monotonic in the above sense. We assign to the reader the task of checking this fact.

Theorem 3.3   (Monotonicity) Let A be any sentence of L. Let $[A]^M$ represent the value of A, at the model M, under the Kleene interpretation of the logical connectives. Then $M \leqslant M'$ implies $[A]^M \leqslant [A]^{M'}$.

Proof By induction on A. For the atomic wff the result follows from the hypothesis that $M \leqslant M'$. For more complex wff the result follows from the monotonicity of the Kleene connectives, for example $[A \ \& \ B]^M = [A]^M \wedge [B]^M$; by induction $[A]^M \leqslant [A]^{M'}$ and $[B]^M \leqslant [B]^{M'}$, and so by the monotonicity of $\wedge$ we have $[A]^M \wedge [B]^M \leqslant [A]^{M'} \vee [B]^{M'}$ as required.

A similar result actually holds for Bochvar's connectives. So that under either Kleene's or Bochvar's regimes our robot satisfies the above requirement. This is not so under the administration of Lukasiewicz. For example, the conditional operator $\rightarrow$ is not monotonic: if $p = q = i$ then $p \rightarrow q = t$, but if $p = t$ and $q = i$ then $p \rightarrow q = i$. Hence the proof breaks down in the conditional case.

So both Bochvar's logic and that of Kleene satisfy the monotonicity constraint; the behaviour of our robot can be described by either. The difference is simply that the Kleene-robot decides on the truth-value of a sentence where it can (for example, if $p = t$ and $q = u$ then $p \vee q = t$) but Bochvar's robot does not.

Our robots are very well-behaved animals. They never jump to any unwarranted conclusions, and they only store in their data bases things they are sure of, and subsequently, they see no necessity to revise their beliefs. Such a robot would not be useless but would, in some respects, be less useful than one prepared to carry out such revisions. In Chapter 5 we shall implicitly consider such a robot and the logic governing its behaviour. In doing so, we shall develop a logic which extends 3-valued logic by allowing the robot to jump to conclusions which are not strictly sanctioned by the semantic machinery of 3-valued logic. This will lead us directly into the area of so-called non-monotonic reasoning.

3.4 STRICTNESS

In the previous section we claimed that only the Bochvar and Kleene interpretations of the connectives make computational sense, the crucial issue being that of monotonicity. In this section we look more closely at the computational difference between these two logics. The central idea is the following.

Definition 4.1 A truth-function $F: \{t, f, u\}^n \to \{t, f, u\}$ will be said to be *strict in its ith argument* $(1 \leqslant i \leqslant n)$ iff for each $d_1, \ldots, d_n$ in $\{t, f, u\}^n$ with $d_i = u$, $F(d_0, \ldots, d_n) = u$. If F is strict in all its arguments we shall say it is *strict*.

Consider an implementation of Boolean expressions involving strict connectives. If any subexpression receives the undefined value then the whole expression will receive that value. This is, for example, the evaluation mechanism employed in the regime of call by value. Bochvar's connectives are strict in the above sense, whereas not all Kleene's connectives are. We can, however, always turn a non-strict connective into a strict one by employing the following device. Define

Strict: $(\{t, f, u\}^n \to \{t, f, u\}) \to (\{t, f, u\}^n \to \{t, f, u\})$
by

$$\text{Strict } (F)\,(d_1, \ldots, d_n) = \begin{cases} u & - \text{ if any } d_i = u,\ 1 \leqslant i \leqslant n \\ F(d_1, \ldots, d_n) & - \text{ otherwise} \end{cases}$$

It is clear that the function *strict* sends the Kleene connectives to the Bochvar connectives. Kleene's connectives, therefore, seem to be more appropriate to an implementation corresponding to call by name rather than call by value.

Our strict robot is a cautious creature; where there is any uncertainty it remains silent.

BIBLIOGRAPHICAL NOTES

The best informal discussion of three-valued logics is to be found in Haack (1974), (1978). The author provides a very thorough discussion of the philosophical foundations of the subject. Kleene (1952) is the original source for both the strong and weak system of Kleene. Luckasiewicz (1920) is still the best account of Lukasiewicz's logics. Bochvar's logics can be found in Bochvar (1939). Rosser & Turquette (1958) is a good general introduction to many-valued logics. Most of the original papers can be found in McCall (1967). Dunn and Epstein (1975) contain some useful papers as regards applications of such logics.

Bochvar, D. (1939) 'On three-valued logical calculus and its application to the analysis of contradictions', in: *Matematiceskij Sbornik* **4** 353–369.

Dunn, J. H. & Epstein, G. (1975) *Modern uses of multiple-valued logics.* D. Reidel Pub. Co. Invited Papers from the 5th International Symposium on Multiple—valued Logic.

Haack, S. (1974) *Deviant logic,* Cambridge Univ. Press.

Haack, S. (1978) *Philosophy of logics,* Cambridge Univ. Press.

Kleene, S. (1952) *Introduction of metamathematics,* Van Nostrand.

Lukasiewicz, J. (1920) 'On 3-valued logic', in: McCall, S. *Polish logic* (Oxford U. P. 1967).

Lukasiewicz, J. (1930) 'Many-valued systems of propositonal logic', in McCall, S. *Polish logic* (Oxford U. P. 1967).

McCall, S. (1967) *Polish logic 1920—1939* Oxford U. P.

Reichenbach, H. (1944) *Philosophical foundations of quantum mechanics,* California U. P.

Rosser, J. B. & Turquette, A. R. (1958) *Many-valued logics.* Amsterdam, North Holland.

4

Intuitionistic logic:
Martin-Löf's theory of types

4.1 INTUITIONISM

This chapter is devoted to intuitionistic logic (and mathematics) and to one particular application of it to computer science. The application alluded to is Martin-Löf's theory of types. Indeed, it is somewhat of a misnomer to refer to the theory of types as an application since it presents us with a unified framework in which to implement the activity of program specification, construction, and verification. Much of this chapter is given over to an exposition of Martin-Löf's theory, but first it seems prudent to say a little about the intuitionistic conception of logic and mathematics.

For both Frege and Russell, and for classical logicians generally, logic is the most fundamental, and general, of all theories. This idea is basic, for example, to the logistic program since, according to it, mathematics was in need of a justification from below, and this justification was to be supplied by logic itself. Intuitionists, on the other hand, draw a different moral from the fact that classical mathematics is in need of justification. In their view, mathematics is primary and logic secondary: logic is nothing more than a collection of rules discovered, *a posteriori*, which happen to characterise the inference patterns implicit in mathematics when correctly practised. The phrase 'correctly practised' is significant since, in addition to their radical views about the relationship between mathematics and logic, they hold a rather unusual view about the nature of mathematics itself. First, numbers are mental entities. According to Brouwer, they are constructed out of 'the sensation of time'. Mathematics is essentially a mental activity. Secondly, only 'constructable' objects are legitimate in intuitionistic mathematics. This rules out, for example, almost all of the cumulative hierarchy of sets. Indeed, intuitionism admits no completed infinite totalities which are not, in some sense, constructable. Moreover, all proofs of mathematical assertions must be constructive. This view has a somewhat debilitating effect upon mathematics; certainly, not all classical mathematics is intuitionistically acceptable. Indeed, before Bishop's contribution (Bishop 1967) many of the results of classical analysis appeared to be intuitionisitically unobtainable.

What impact does this view have upon logic itself? Given that logic is viewed as a secondary enterprise, and that logic is meant to reflect correct mathematical practice, it is not surprising that the impact is considerable. For example, consider the assertion

$$(\exists n) \, (n \text{ is an odd perfect number}).$$

This assertion will be provable only if we are able to *construct* a number which is both odd and perfect. It will be disprovable if its assumption leads, via a *constructive proof,* to a contradiction. But since we neither have a way of constructing such a number, nor can we establish by constructive means that its assumption leads to a contradiction, the assertion is intuitionistically problematic. Such considerations lead intuitionists to reject the law of excluded middle, $A \vee \sim A$, which is a fundamental law of classical logic.

Both in his book and his other writing Dummett has supplied us with a somewhat different perspective on the nature of the disagreement between intuitionists and classical logicians. Dummett's exposition relates to the different theories of meaning employed by the two schools. For the classical mathematician the meaning of any sentence is to be provided by its truth-conditions. This, for example, is reflected in Tarski's account of the semantics for the predicate calculus. The assumption underlying classical mathematics and logic is that the mathematical assertions are determinately either true or false. Intuitionism rejects such a view of meaning. For the intuitionist the meaning of a statement resides not in its truth-conditions but rather in its means of verification or proof. This distinction is reflected in the account of the logical operators provided in the next section. Their meaning is not furnished by truth-conditions, as in almost every other chapter in this book, but by specifying what is to count as a proof of a sentence containing them.

This section is obviously not intended as an exposition of the philosophical foundations of intuitionism. We have only attempted to give the reader sufficient background to follow our exposition of Martin-Löf's theory. For a detailed discussion of the philosophical foundations of intuitionism the reader can do no better than consult Dummett's excellent book.

4.2 THE INTUITIONISTIC INTERPRETATION OF THE LOGICAL CONSTANTS

Classically, the meaning of each logical constant is furnished by specifying the truth-conditions for any sentence in which that constant is the main connective. Intuitionistically, the meaning of each logical constant is to be gleaned from a specification of what is to count as a *proof* for any sentence involving the constant as its main connective. We summarise the intuitionistic meaning of the various logical constants in the following table.

A PROOF OF	CONSISTS OF
$A \vee B$	A proof of A or a proof of B
$A \& B$	A proof of A and a proof of B
$A \to B$	A construction which transforms any given proof of A into a proof of B
$\sim A$	A proof of $A \to \perp$ where $\perp$ is some absurd statement, for example $(0 = 1)$
$\exists x\, A(x)$	A construction of $A(c)$ for some individual c
$\forall x\, A(x)$	A construction which when applied to any individual c yields a proof of $A(c)$

This guide is quite terse, so let's see if we can improve matters a little.

(i) *Disjunction*

A proof of $A \vee B$ is to consist of a proof of A or a proof of B together, presumably, with an indication of which. So that the set of proofs of $A \vee B$, $P(A \vee B)$, can be represented as the *disjoint union* of $P(A)$ and $P(B)$, where $P(A)$ is the set of proofs of A etc. We shall write the disjoint union of $P(A)$ and $P(B)$ as $P(A) + P(B)$. The elements of $P(A) + P(B)$ are, therefore, of the form $i(a)$ and $j(b)$ where $a \in P(A)$ and $b \in P(B)$ and i, j are the injection functions, $i : P(A) \to P(A) + P(B)$ and $j : P(B) \to P(A) + P(B)$.

(ii) *Conjuction*

A proof of A & B is to consist of a pair whose first component is a proof of A and whose second component is a proof of B. In other words, the set of proofs of A & B is to consist of the *cartesian product* of $P(A)$ and $P(B)$, denoted by $P(A) \times P(B)$.

(iii) *Implication*

According to the table a proof of $A \rightarrow B$ is to consist of a construction which when applied to a proof of A yields a proof of B. Put differently, $P(A \rightarrow B)$ is the set of constructions (constructive functions) which when applied to elements of $P(A)$ yield elements of $P(B)$. The set $P(A \rightarrow B)$ is, therefore, the *function space* of constructive functions from $P(A)$ to $P(B)$, which we denote by $P(A) \rightarrow P(B)$.

(iv) *Negation*

Negation is defined in terms of implication. To prove A it is sufficient to prove that A leads to a contradiction. Thus, $P(\sim A)$ is the set of constructive functions from $P(A)$ to $P(\perp)$, where $P(\perp)$ is the empty type.

(v) *Existenial quantification*

A proof of $\exists x A(x)$ consists of an individual c and a proof of $A(c)$. (Strictly speaking, one should also insist that c is given by some construction. We shall return to this point later.) $P(\exists x A(x))$, therefore, consists of ordered pairs $\langle c, d \rangle$ where c is an individual and d is a proof of $A(c)$. Alternatively, $P(\exists x A(x))$ is *the disjoint union* of the family $\exists (A(c))$, indexed by the domain of individuals C. We write this disjoint union as $(\Sigma\, c \in C)\, P(A(c))$.

(vi) *Universal quantification*

A proof of $\forall x A(x)$ is a construction or effective function which when applied to an individual c yields a proof of $A(c)$. The set $P(\forall x A(x))$ is thus the *cartesian product of the family* $P(A(c))$, indexed by the domain of individuals C. We write this cartesian product as $(\mathbb{T}\, c \in C)\, (P(A(c))$.

We can summarise all this quite succinctly as follows:

$$
\begin{aligned}
P(A \vee B) &= P(A) + P(B) \\
P(A\ \&\ B) &= P(A) \times P(B) \\
P(A \rightarrow B) &= P(A) \rightarrow P(B) \\
P(\exists x A(x)) &= (\Sigma\, c \in C)\, P(A(c)) \\
P(\forall x A(x)) &= (\mathbb{T}\, c \in C)\, P(A(c))
\end{aligned}
$$

This should have made things somewhat more explicit, but there are still two areas of vagueness. Firstly, what exactly is a construction or constructive function, and what constitutes a domain of individuals or a domain of quantification? Martin-Löf supplies an answer to these questions in terms of his theory of types.

The theory of types was developed as a formalisation of constructive mathematics. It is intended to be a full-scale system for formalising intuitionistic mathematics developed, for example, in Bishop (1967). The language of the theory sanctions the occurrence of proofs within propositions, and as a consequence propositions can express properties of proofs. This facility has important consequences for the theory of types as a programming language. We now re-examine the intuitionistic meaning of the logical constants and deploy the discussion to introduce Martin-Löf's theory.

Let A be any proposition. The set $P(A)$ is the set of proofs of A which, following Martin-Löf, we shall refer to as *the objects of type A*. Martin-Löf, influenced by the work of Curry, Howard, and Scott, takes the very natural step of *identifying types with propositions*. What implications does this identification have for the meaning of the logical constants?

In the case of disjunction we must identify $A \vee B$ with $P(A + B)$, but since $P(A + B) = P(A) + P(B)$ and, by induction, $P(A)$ is to be identified with A and $P(B)$ with B, we are to identify the proposition $A \vee B$ with the *disjoint union $A + B$*. Similarly, $A \mathrel{\&} B$ is to be identified with the *cartesian product $A \times B$*. For implication we must identify the proposition $A \to B$ with $[A \to B]$, the *type of functions* from A to B. As regards negation, the proposition $\sim A$ is identified with $A \to \phi$, where ϕ is the empty type.

This brings us to consider the quantifiers. Earlier, we raised a question about the nature of domains of quantification. In intuitionistic mathematics quantification is restricted to those domains which are 'graspable' (to borrow a phrase of Dummett's). For Martin-Löf, domains of quantification are types. Subsequently, we never employ an unrestricted quantifier, but rather quantifications of the form $\exists x \in A$ or $\forall x \in A$, to be understood as 'there exists an object of type A' and 'for all objects of type A', respectively. We must now modify our account of the quantifiers to allow for this refinement.

A proof of $(\exists x \in A) B(x)$ consists of a pair $\langle a, b \rangle$ whose first component is an object of type A and whose second is a proof of $B(a)$. In other words, $P((\exists x \in A) B(x))$ is the disjoint union of the family $P(B(a))$, indexed by the elements of type A. Under the identification of propositions with types this means we are to identify

$(\exists x \in A) B (x)$ with the *disjoint union* $(\Sigma x \in A) B (x)$. Universal quantification is to undergo a similar transformation. A proof of $(\forall x \in A) B (x)$ is an effective function which to each object a of type A yields an object of type $B (a)$. Put differently, $P ((\forall x \in A) B (x))$ is the cartesian product of the family $P (B (a))$, indexed by the type A. Employing the identification we are instructed to identify the proposition $(\forall x \in A) B (x)$ with the *cartesian product* $(\Pi x \in A) B (x)$.

We have addressed the question concerning domains of quantification but have said nothing about the definition of constructions/constructive functions. Martin-Löf supplies a precise account of such functions by employing inference rules (in a natural deduction system) which specify what the objects of each type are. We shall return shortly to the issue of how the types, and the objects of the various types, are specified.

The reader should now possess some idea of what the theory of types involves. In the next two sections we cover the ground in more detail, and in the final section we discuss its application to computer science. We begin by discussing the language of the theory of types. This comes in two intimately related parts: the language of the types themselves and the language of the objects of the various types.

4.3 THE LANGUAGE OF THE THEORY OF TYPES

Essentially, expressions in the theory of types are built up from variables and constants by means of application and functional abstraction. The language is not, however, type-free in the sense of the lambda calculus. There are further restrictions on what forms of expression are well-formed. Nordström & Smith (1983) use the notion of 'arity' to impose the appropriate restrictions on which forms of application are legitimate. Roughly, the arity of an expression describes the functionality of the expression, in that it indicates the arity of the expressions to which it can meaningfully be applied. A *saturated* expression is one that cannot be applied to anything.

We now describe the language of expressions a little more precisely. In doing so we follow the presentation in Nordström & Smith (1983).

1. A variable is an expression
2. A constant is an expression
3. If $e_1, \ldots, e_n$ are expressions of appropriate arities then the application $e(e_1, \ldots, e_n)$ is an expression. The intention here is that the arity of e must be such that it can be applied to expressions having the arity of the expressions $e_1, \ldots, e_n$.

4. If $x_1, \ldots, x_n$ are variables and e is an expression, then the abstraction $(x_1, \ldots, x_n)e$ is an expression. The resulting expression possesses an arity which is such that, when it is applied to an expression having the same arity as the variables $x_1, \ldots, x_n$, it yields an expression with the same arity as e.

Constants come in two kinds: primitive constants and defined constants. Examples of the former are $\circ$, succ, λ (λ-abstraction operator). Defined constants are introduced by explicit definitions like

$$f(x_1, \ldots, x_n) = b$$

where the constant f is introduced and, f when applied to the variables $x_1, \ldots, x_n$, is definitionally equal to b. This is much like functional defintion in programming languages.

It will be constructive to consider a few examples in more detail. Consider the expressions $(\Sigma\, x \in A)\, B$ and $(\Pi\, x \in A)\, B$ introduced in section 4.2. To conform to the above description we need to present these as applications and/or abstractions. The expression $(\Sigma\, x \in A)\, B$ actually consists of two parts: an expression denoting a type A and an expression of the form $(x)\, B\,(x)$, in which the variable x is bound. In conformity to the above syntax the expression should be written as $\Sigma\,(A, (x)\, B\, x))$. Similarly, $(\Pi\, x \in A)\, B$ should be recast as $\Pi\,(A, (x)\, B\,(x))$. In what follows, however, we shall frequently employ the more familiar notation for many expressions.

We now provide a list of some of the more common forms of expression to be found in the theory of types.

Canonical	Non-canonical
$\Pi\,(A, (x)\, B\,(x)), (\lambda x)\, b$	$c\,(a)$
$\Sigma\,(A, (x)\, B\,(x)), (a, b)$	$(Exy)\,(c, d)$
$+\,(A, b), i\,(a), j\,(b)$	$(Dxy)\,(c, d, e)$
$I\,(A, a, b), r$	$J\,(c, d)$

The terms 'canonical' and 'non-canonical' employed in the above table relate to the meaning of expressions in the theory of types. Both in classical mathematics (logic) and computer science the meaning of an expression or a program is provided by an associated semantic definition. In classical first-order logic, for example, the semantics is provided via the notion of a model and Tarski's notion of satisfaction. In programming languages one standard definitional technique employs the semantic domains of Dana Scott's theory of computation. Implicit in both is the assumption that the meaning of a syntactic object is to be furnished via certain mathematical structures which ultimately have their existence guaranteed by the ontology of standard Zermelo-Fraenkel set theory (Krivine 1971). Type theory is intended to be a foundation for constructive mathematics and it is, therefore, just perverse to demand an explanation of the language of type theory in set-theoretical terms. Instead, in type theory the meaning of an expression is provided by a rule of computation.

The mechanical procedure of computing the value of an expression is called *evaluation*. An expression which has itself as a value is called *canonical* or normal. An expression which is not canonical is called *non-canonical*. The value of a non-canonical expression $f(e_1, \ldots, e_n)$ is a canonical expression obtained by following the computation rules for the constant f. In type theory only the form f of an expression $f(e_1, \ldots, e_n)$ determines whether the expression is canonical or not. So, for example, succ (e) is canonical regardless of the form of e. The reason for this concerns the nature of evaluation. In general, it is not feasible to require all parts $e_1, \ldots, e_n$ of a canonical expression to be evaluated since some parts of the expression may have no value. An expression is *fully evaluated* if it is canonical and all saturated parts are fully evaluated.

To illustrate the process of evaluation we indicate how the non-canonical expressions in our table are to be evaluated.

To execute an expression of the $e_1(e_2)$ we first execute e_1. If we obtain $(\lambda x)b$ as a result, we continue by executing $b(e_2|x)$ (that is, b with e_2 substituted for x). To execute or evaluate $(Exy)(c, d)$ we first execute c. If (a, b) results, we execute $d(a, b|x, y)$ (substitute a for x and b for y in d). To evaluate $D(x, y)(c, d, e)$ we first execute c. If we get $i(a)$ as a result, we execute $d(a|x)$. If, alternatively, we get $j(b)$ as the result of executing c, we excute $e(b|y)$ instead. To execute $J(c, d)$ we first execute c. If r results we execute d.

In summary, expressions in the theory of types are constructed from variables and constants by means of abstraction and application. The meaning is not provided by means of an associated semantic definition but by means of rules of evaluation.

4.4 JUDGEMENTS AND RULES OF INFERENCE

The heart of Martin-Löf's theory is concerned with making judgements of the form

  (i) A is a type
  (ii) A and B are equal types

(iii) a is an object of type A

(iv) a and b are equal objects of type A

which are abbreviated as (i) A type, (ii) $A = B$, (iii) $a \in A$, and (iv) $a = b \in A$ respectively. Types may be identified with sets, propositions, or tasks. Consequently, each of the four types of judgement admits to three different intuitive readings. The third judgement, for example, can be understood as

> a is an element of the set A,
>
> a is a proof of the proposition A,
>
> a is a program for the task A.

It is, of course, the third interpretation which is relevant to computer science. These readings are only meant as an aid to our understanding; they are not intended to fix the meanings of the various forms of judgement in any formal sense. This is achieved by the inference rules of the system and, in particular, the so-called introduction rules.

In Martin-Löf (1982) canonical types are specified in the following way:

> A canonical type A is defined by prescribing how a canonical object of type A is formed as well as how two equal canonical object of type A are formed.

Such prescriptions are supplied by the introduction rules for the various types. For example, consider the cartesian product construction on types introduced in section 4.2. According to the above explanation we need to supply a rule for prescribing how a canonical object of type A is formed as well as one which displays how two equal canonincal objects of type A are formed. The relevant rules Martin-Löf calls $\prod$ -*introduction*.

$$
\frac{
\begin{array}{c} (x \in A) \\ b \in B \end{array}
}{
(\lambda x)b \in (\textstyle\prod x \in A)B
}
\qquad
\frac{
\begin{array}{c} (x \in A) \\ b = d \in B \end{array}
}{
(\lambda x)b = (\lambda x)d \in (\textstyle\prod x \in A)B
}
$$

The bracketed expression $(x \in A)$ represents a premise or assumption, and, in general, judgements in the theory of types are made relative to such assumptions. We refer the reader to Martin-Löf (1982) for details.

As a further illustration consider the rule(s) for the disjoint union construction (Σ-introduction):

$$a \in A \quad b \in B(a|x) \qquad\qquad a = c \in A \quad b = d \in B(a|x)$$

$$\overline{} \qquad\qquad \overline{}$$

$$(a, b) \in (\Sigma\, x \in A)B \qquad\quad (a, b) = (c, d) \in (\Sigma\, x \in A)B$$

The first rule stipulates how a canonical object of $(\Sigma\, x \in A)B$ is formed, while the second informs us how two equal objects of the types are formed. In all these rules the equality relation between objects is required to be an equivalence relation.

Such definitions of the canonical types enable us to provide a more formal account of the various judgements. For example, a judgement of the form A type means that A has a canonical type as value, whereas the judgement $a = b \in A$ means that a and b, when evaluated, have equal canonical objects of the canonical type denoted by A as values. This definition makes perfect sense since, by assumption, A has a canonical type as value (this is what it means to be a type by the previous definition) and by the definition of canonical types we know how two canonical objects of the same type are formed.

A second kind of inference rule in the system is a 'mirror-image' of the introduction rule. Again we illustrate by reference to the cartesian product construction for types.

$$\Pi\text{-Elimination}$$

$$c \in (\Pi\, x \in A)B \quad a \in A \qquad c = f \in (\Pi\, x \in A)B \quad a = d \in A$$

$$\overline{} \qquad\qquad \overline{}$$

$$c\,(a) \in B(a|x) \qquad\qquad c(a) = f(d) \in B(a|x)$$

As before, there are two parts to the elimination rules, the first informs us how to form an application, and the second how two equal applications are formed. These rules were implicit in our discussion of universal quantification: the expression c denotes a function which to each element of type A assigns an object $c\,(a)$ of type $B(a|x)$.

There are similar rules governing the disjoint union and cartesian product two types, finite types and the type of natural numbers. If additional types are added (for example enumeration types, lists etc.) then rules governing these types are added as required. In addition to the rules for the various types, Martin-Löf's system includes more general rules relating to equality of objects and types (for example, they have to be equivalence relations).

As an illustration of his theory Martin-Löf offers a proof of the axiom of choice. He begins with the premises

A type
B type $(x \in A)$
C type $(x \in A, y \in B)$

Using the abbreviation $A \to B$ for $(\mathbb{T} x \in A) B$ (x not free in B), the expression E,

$$(\mathbb{T} x \in A) (\Sigma y \in B) C \to (\Sigma f \in (\mathbb{T} x \in A) B) (\mathbb{T} x \in A) C (f(x), y)$$

is a type which, when understood as a proposition, expresses the axiom of choice. Using the proof rules and the above assumptions he ends up with a conclusion of the form

$$(\lambda z) ((\lambda x) p (z(x)), (\lambda x) q (z (x))) \in E.$$

Basically, the strategy of the proof is to employ the elimination rules to break down the antecedent of the expression E, and the introduction rules to build up the consequent. The expression

$$(\lambda z) ((\lambda x) p (z (x)), (\lambda x) q (z (x)))$$

constitutes the required proof of the axiom of choice.

4.5 THE THEORY OF TYPES AS A PROGRAMMING LANGUAGE

The relevance of Per Martin-Löf's theory to computer science relates to the third form of judgements in the theory. Consider the judgement $a \in A$. Under the third interpretation A is to be interpreted as a problem or task (or a *specification* of such) and a is a *program* for its solution. The specification is a type definition, and the program is an object which meets the specification. So the natural separation between expressions which denote types and those which refer to objects of the various types defines a specification language on the one hand and a programming language on the other.

The actual programming language is a purely functional language, and in appearance resembles a version of the lambda calculus. The inference rules, which among other things, define the grammar of this language, do not permit self-application, and so the language has as a basis of polymorphically-typed version of the lambda calculus.

One other significant difference between type theory as a programming language and more conventional languages is that only primitive recursion is allowed. In the theory of types all functions are *total*. Nevertheless, one is permitted to define higher order functions by primitive recursion (see Smith (1982)).

To illustrate the use of the theory of types as both a specification and a programming language we employ an example due to Nordström & Smith (1983). In their example the target program must generate a KWIC index (keyword in context). The program, given a list of titles and a list of the non-significant words, must produce an alphabetically sorted list of the significant rotations of the titles, where a significant rotation is a cyclic rearrangement of the words in which the first word is significant. Nordström & Smith produce a formal specification of this task in the following way.

First they assume that we have certain enumeration types defined, namely *PrintableChar* which is a subset of the enumeration type *Ascii*. They then define via explicit definition.

$$\text{Title} = \text{List (Word)}$$

$$\text{Word} = \text{List (PrintableChar)}$$

A *rotation* of a list is a cyclic rearrangement of the elements in the list which can be defined as

$$\text{rotation } (y, t) = (\exists n \in N) \, (\text{Shift}^n(y) = t)$$

where

$$\text{shift(nil)} = \text{nil}$$
$$\text{shift}(a.s) = s <> (a.\,\text{nil})$$

and

$$f^0(x) = x$$
$$f^{n+1}(x) = f(f^n(x))$$

and $<>$ is the obvious concatenation operator. They then introduce the notion of *significant rotation* by

$$\text{signrot } (y, t, n) = \text{rotation } (y, t) \, \&$$
$$(\text{first } (y) \, \text{in}_{\text{WORD}} \, n)$$

where

$$a \, in_A \, \text{nil} = \perp$$
$$a \, in_A \, b.s = [a =_A b] \vee (a \, in_A \, s)$$

and $\perp$ stands for absurdity, that is, a proposition with no proof.

In the example the output is sorted with respect to a lexicographical ordering, $<_A$, between the titles by

$$\text{lex}(A) (<_A) (\text{nil}, \text{nil}) = T$$
$$\text{lex}(A) (<_A) (a.s, \text{nil}) = \bot$$
$$\text{lex}(A) (<_A) (\text{nil}, b.t) = t$$
$$\text{lex}(A) (<_A) (a.s, b.t) = [a =_A b] \ \& \ \text{lex}(A) (<_A) (s, t)$$
$$\vee$$
$$[a =_A b] \ \& \ (a <_A b)$$

where $T = \{.\}$.

In other words, if $<$ is an ordering between the printable characters, then lex(Printablechar) $(<)$ is an ordering on the words and lex(word) (lex(Printablechar) $(<)$) is an ordering on the titles. In the above, T is the proposition which is always true and is represented as a set with one element.

The proposition Ordered$'$ (x) states that the list of titles is sorted according to a lexicographical ordering and Nordström and Smith define this as follows:

Ordered$'$ $(x) = $ Ordered(Lex(Word) (Lex(Printablechar) $(<)$), x)
where
Ordered $(0, x)$
is defined by
Ordered $(0, \text{nil}) = T$
Ordered $(0, a. \text{nil}) = T$
Ordered $(0, a.b.s) = 0 (a, b) \ \& \ $Ordered $(0, b. s)$

With all this achieved the actual specification is relatively straightforward:

$$E \begin{cases} (\forall t \in \text{List}(\text{Title})) (\forall n \in \text{List}(\text{Word})) \\ (\exists \ x \in \text{List}(\text{Title})) \\ (\text{Ordered}' (x)) \ \& \ (\forall y \in \text{Title}) (y \text{ in } x \leftrightarrow \\ \qquad (\exists z \in \text{Title}) ((z \text{ in } t) \ \& \ \text{Signrot} (y, z, n)))). \end{cases}$$

If we employ the inference machinery of type theory to prove this proposition/specification we obtain a function f whose type is given by the above specification. In other words, we end up with a judgement of the form $f \in E$. Moreover, the function f, when applied to a list of titles t and a list n of words, gives a pair, the first component of which is the required result, that is, p $(ap$ $(ap$ $(f, t), n))$. This provides the KWIC index of t with respect to the list of nonsignificant words n.

The benefits of Martin-Löf's approach are, in principle, quite considerable. Under the umbrella of one theory there exists a specification language, a programming language (which is purely functional in character), and a formal means of deriving programs from their specifications. This derivation process is, of course, not mechanical; one has to construct a proof of a judgement of the form $a \in A$. Nevertheless, the process of constructing the proof not only facilitates the derivation of the program from its specification, but also provides a proof that the derived program meets the specifications. All this should be seen in contrast to the methodology adopted in Hoare-type correctness proofs. In this set-up not only are there two relatively distinct languages (the programming language and the logical language in which the correctness proofs are carried out) but also there is a greater disparity between the processes of program construction and verification. To be fair to the disciples of Hoare-style program construction and verification, we should add that the philosophy behind their approach is to bring together these two processes (for example, the use of invariants in program construction), but it does appear that both the formal tools available and the programming languages to which they are applied tend to mitigate against this aspiration.

In conclusion, Martin-Löf's theory offers an exciting prospect for a unified view of program specification, construction, and verification.

BIBLIOGRAPHICAL NOTES

The best easily available introductions to intuitionism are Heyting (1956) and Dummett (1977). For the theory of types Martin-Löf's papers are a must. The presentations of Nordström & Smith (1983) and Nordström and Petersson (1983) form the basis of our exposition. Smith (1982) uses Martin-Löf's theory to construct a program for the algorithm Quicksort. Nordström (1981) contains a simple example of program derivation from a formal specification.

There are several other approaches to the problem of program specification whose aims and methods are very closely related to those of Martin-Löf. The work of Micheal Beeson at San Jose deserves special mention. His work is based on a formalisation of constructive mathematics due to Feferman. Feferman's system differs from that of Martin-Löf in being 'type-free'. The actual programming language appears to be the classical theory of combinators together with a proof theory based upon Heyting arithmetic. The reader should consult Beeson (1983) for a sketch of the system. The works of Constable and Constable & O'Donnell also pursue a similar theme and cannot be neglected by the serious student of the subject.

Beeson, M. (1984) 'Proving programs and programming proofs', in: *Proc. 7th Int. Cong. of Logic, Methodology and Philosophy of Science,* Salzburg. Forthcoming in 'Logic, methodology and the philosphy of science', North Holland Studies in Logic.

Bishop, E. (1967) 'Mathematics as a numerical language', in: *Intuitionism and proof theory,* ed. Myhill, Kino, & Vesley. North Holland Studies in Logic, Amsterdam, 53–71.

de Bruijn, N. G. (1980) 'A survey of the project Automath', in: *To H. B. Curry: Essays on combinatory logic, lambda calculus and formalism,* ed. Seldin, J. P. & Hindley, J. R., Academic Press, London.

Constable, R. L. (1971) 'Constructive mathematics and automatic program writers', in: *Proc. IFIP Congress 1971,* North Holland.

Constable, R. L. (1983) 'Partial functions in constructive formal theories'. In: *Theoretical computer science.* Springer Lecture Notes in Computer Science, Vol 145 1–19. ed. A. B. Cremers & H. P. Kriegel.

Constable, R. L. (1983) 'Constructive mathematics as a programming logic I: some principles of the theory', in: *Foundations of computer science* 1983. Springer Lecture Notes in Computer Science, Vol 158, 64–78 ed. Marek Karpinski.

Constable, R. L. (1983) 'Mathematics as programming': in: *Logics of programs,* Springer Lecture Notes in Computer Science. Vol 164. ed. E. Clarke & d. Kozen, 116–129.

Constable, R. L. & O'Donnell, M. J. (1978) *A programming logic,* Winthrop, Cambridge, Mass.

Dummett, M. (1977) *Elements of intuitionism,* Oxford U. P.

Heyting, A. (1956) *Intuitionism, an introduction,* North Holland.

Howard, W. A. (1980) 'The formulae-as-type notion of construction', in; *To H. B. Curry: essays on combinatory logic, lambda calculus and formalism,* ed. Seldin, J. P. & Hindley, J. R., Academic Press, London, 429–441.

Krivine, J. L. (1971) 'Introduction to axiomatic set theory', D. Reidel Pub. Company.

Martin-Löf, P. (1975) 'An intuitionistic theory of types: predicative part', in: *Logic colloquium 1973,* ed. Rose, H. E. & Shephedson, J. C., North Holland, Amsterdam, 73–118.

Martin-Löf, P. (1982) 'Constructive mathematics and computer Programming', in Logic, Methodology and philosophy of science,

VI *(Proc. of the 6th Int. Cong., Hannover, 1979),* North Holland Publishing Company, Amsterdam, 153–175.

Nordström, B. (1981) 'Programming in constructive set theory: some examples', *Proc. 1981 ACM Conference on Functional Programming Languages and Computer Architecture.* Portsmouth, New Hampshire 48–54.

Nordström, B. & Smith, J. (1983) 'Why type theory for programming? a short introduction', in *Proc. Declarative Programming Workshop,* University College, London. Available from Dept. of Computer Science, University College, London. Available also as: *Computer Science Memo 80.* Programming Methodology Group, Dept. of Computer Sciences, University of Göteborg, S–412 96 Göteborg, Sweden.

Nordström, B. & Petersson, K. (1983) 'Types and specifications' in: *Information Processing 83.* ed. R.E.A. Mason, Elsevier Science Publishers, North Holland, 915–920.

Scott, D. (1970) 'Constructive validity', in: *Symposium on Automatic Demonstration, Lecture Notes in Mathematics,* Vol 125. Springer Verlag, Berlin, 169–176.

Smith, J. (1982) 'The identification of propositions and types in Martin-Löf's type theory: a programming example', in *Foundations of computation theory,* Springer Lecture Notes in Computer Science. No 158. ed. M. Karpinski, 445–454.

5

Towards a semantic theory of non-monotonic inference

5.1 NON-MONOTONIC REASONING

The phenomenon of non-monotonic inference is, I think, best illustrated by way of example, and we can do no better than steal one from Dov Gabbay (1982). The World Travel Agency (WTA) offers package tours from New York to Paris and Stuttgart. Every Sunday passengers board a WTA plane in New York; some passengers disembark in Paris, while others continue to Stuttgart. The Stuttgart office arranges for hotels in Europe. At 12.00, Stuttgart office learns that all flights into Paris are to be rerouted — apparently some nasty terrorists have taken Paris airport by storm. Stuttgart has to decide what to do with the WTA group. They cannot contact New York because all telephone lines are engaged. The only established fact is that the WTA plane left New York, presumably on schedule. The Stuttgart office reasons that the WTA plane will be rerouted to London; the Paris passengers will disembark and the remainder proceed to Stuttgart. Gabbay represents this reasoning as follows.

(a) *Established at 12.00 hours Stuttgart time:*
   A = Group flight took-off.
   B = Terrorist attack on Paris airport.

(b) *Assumed true at 12.00 hours on basis of company procedures and no evidence to the contrary:*
   $C =$ Flight rerouted to Heathrow.

(c) *Conclusion at 12.00:*
   $D =$ The Stuttgart passengers are arriving tonight from London.

As this nail-biting drama unfolds the unexpected occurs. At 14.00 the resourceful Stuttgart office manages to establish a telephone link with New York. What they learn causes some concern; the plane was two and a half hours late in take-off. This changes the picture considerably. The Stuttgart office now reasons (in consultation with New York) that the Captain, when hearing of the Paris attack, decided to return the short distance to New York. This reasoning is best summarised in the following way.

(a') *Established time at 14.00:*
   A, B and
   $(A') =$ Take-off delayed in New York.

(b') *Assumed true on the basis of company procedures, and no evidence to the contrary:*
   $(C') =$ Flight returning to New York.

(c') *Conclusion at 14.00*
   $\sim D =$ Stuttgart passengers not arriving from London tonight.

To formalise this reasoning assume that we have at our disposal the predicate calculus, and some standard notion of provability $\vdash$ (for example, classical first-order provability).

At 12.00 the Stuttgart office reasons as follows:

(a)   We know $A \& B$ and assume C.
(b) $A \& B \& C \vdash D$
(c) $A \& B$ are sufficient to 'non-monotonically' infer D.

At 14.00 hours the picture is somewhat different

(a') We know $A \& B \& A'$ and assume C'.
(b') $A \& B \& A' \& C' \vdash \sim D$
(c') $A \& B \& A'$ are sufficient to 'non-monotonically' infer $\sim D$.

This example brings out quite clearly the nature of non-monotonic inference. At 12.00 the Stuttgart office made what seemed to them (given the information at their disposal) certain plausible assumptions, and these assumptions permitted certain inferences to be drawn. Unfortunately, the assumptions turned out to be less than plausible given the additional information. Subsequently, conclusion

D was no longer warranted. *'Non-monotonic' logical systems are logics in which the introduction of new information (axioms) can invalidate old theorems.* So in our example, prior to the information A', D was provable, but after A' was added, $\sim D$ turned out to be provable. In other words, a relation of inference $\vdash$ is *monotonic* if for each pair of theories (set of sentences) S_1 and S_2 if $S_1 \subseteq S_2$ then $\text{Th}(S_1) \subseteq \text{Th}(S_2)$ where $\text{Th}(S_1) = \{A : S_1 \vdash A\}$; otherwise $\vdash$ is non-monotonic.

As McDermott & Doyle (1980) point out, this phenomenon of 'non-monotonicity' is ubiquitous, if implicit, in Artificial Intelligence. For example, studies of visual perception and knowledge representation embody mechanisms, of one form or another, whose task is to compensate for the taking of incorrect, even if seemingly appropriate, decisions. Such behaviour implicitly involves a form of reasoning which is essentially 'non-monotonic'. The possibility of failure may lead to the revision of certain assumptions and the subsequent rejection of certain conclusions.

AI programs are thus forced to take decisions in the light of incomplete information. Much practical work has been done to circumvent this difficulty. For example, PLANNER (Hewitt 1973) attempted to cope with such non-monotonic inference by introducing a new primitive called THNOT. This operator, given a goal A, succeeded only if the goal A failed; otherwise the goal THNOT(A) failed. Sanderwell (1972) introduced the primitive UNLESS into the predicate calculus with the intended meaning that UNLESS (A) was to be asserted in case A was not deducible as a theorem of the predicate calculus.

It is not our intention to dig deeply into any specific AI application. McDermott & Doyle's paper lists a host of areas where non-monotonic reasoning is utilised, if only implicitly. Our intention is to examine, in the spirit of McDermott & Doyle, the foundations of the subject of non-monotonic reasoning, and, hopefully to put it on a sound semantic footing. In the next section we shall scrutinize the work of McDermott & Doyle; in the following section we shall examine that of Dov Gabbay and then sketch an approach of our own. Finally, we consider a recent contribution due to Bob Moore called 'autoepistemic logic'.

5.2 NON-MONOTONIC MODAL THEORIES

One of the first attempts to systematically develop a logic for non-monotonic reasoning was made by Drew McDermott & Jon Doyle.

In McDermott & Doyle (1980) we are presented with a version of the predicate calculus which, in addition to the standard operators of the predicate calculus, also admits a certain operator 'M' which is intended to signify some assertion of 'consistency'. In this original presentation of their system this operator is given no explicit semantics. This omission is rectified, however, in a more recent publication due to McDermott (1982). Our objective in this section is to provide a brief exposition and critique of their approach, and in this regard we shall largely concentrate on the presentation given in this later paper.

The language that McDermott studies is actually that of first-order modal logic, but to avoid confusion with Chapter 2 we shall refer to it here as L_N. Moreover, the semantics McDermott supplies is essentially that of Chapter 2, although the intended interpretation of the operator M is, as we shall see, somewhat different. For convenience and completeness we repeat the main definition.

Definition 1.1 A *modal frame M* for L_N is a structure $\langle W, D, R, F \rangle$ where
(i) W is a non-empty set (of 'possible worlds');
(ii) D is a non-empty set;
(iii) R is a binary relation of 'accessibility' between elements of W;
(iv) F is a function which assigns to each pair, consisting of an n-place function symbol ($n \geqslant 0$) and an element of W, a function from D^n to D, and to each pair, consisting of an n-place relation symbol ($n > 0$) and an element of W, and element of 2^{D^n}.

The semantics for L_N is given exactly as in Chapter 2 by recursively defining the relation $M \models_{g,w} A$ which is intended to convey the information that the assignment function g *satisfies* the wff A, at the world w, in the frame M. We refer the reader to Chapter 2 for the details. As we pointed out there, different restrictions on the accessibility relation lead to different underlying modal logics. For example, where the relation R, of accessibility, is reflexive we obtain the modal logic T; where R is reflexive and transitive we obtain $S4$, and if R is actually an equivalence relation then we obtain the logic $S5$. Consequently, we obtain three classes of models and three notions of semantic entailment: $\models_T$, $\models_{S4}$, $\models_{S5}$. For example, we shall write $S \models_{T4} A$ (where S is a set of sentences of L_N and A is a sentence) iff for each modal frame M, in which R is reflexive and transitive, and each $w \in W$ we have: if $M \models_{g,w} B$ for each B in S, then $M \models_{w,g} A$ (observe that g is irrelevant here since we are dealing with sentences).

McDermott obtains the obvious completeness results for these three notions of semantic entailment, and so we can, if we wish, view $\models_T$, $\models_{S4}$, $\models_{S5}$ as being characterised proof-theoretically.

This then is the basic semantic framework upon which McDermott builds a theory of non-monotonic inference. Actually, the account of non-monotonic inference proffered by McDermott (1982) is much the same as that of the earlier paper. The only difference concerns the underlying notion of *monotonic* inference: in the earlier paper it was classical first-order entailment; in the later presentation it is $\models_T$, $\models_{S4}$, or $\models_{S5}$.

The idea behind their account of non-monotonic inference is best made clear by considering the following tentative rule of inference:

> Possibilitation (Pos) : 'Can't infer A' then MA.

The notion of inference in the phrase 'can't infer' is not to be identified with any of the relations $\models_T$, $\models_{S4}$, $\models_{S5}$, of modal logic. Rather it is to be somehow obtained from such a relation by some bootstrapping process; we require a relation of entailment, $\mathbin{\vdash\!\!\!\sim}$ which satisfies

$$\nvdash \sim A \text{ then } \mathbin{\vdash\!\!\!\sim} MA.$$

The clearest account of how they achieve this is given in Davis (1980). We begin with an enumeration $\{A_i : i = 1, 2, 3, \ldots\}$ of the wffs of L_N. Let S be some set of premises and $\models$ some underlying notion of entailment (for example $\models_T$, $\models_{S4}$, $\models_{S5}$). Then put

$$S_0 = S$$

and

$$S_{i+1} = \begin{cases} L_N & \text{— if for some } B \text{ in } L_N \\ & \quad MB \in S_i \text{ and } S_i \models \sim B \\ S_i \cup \{MB_i\} & \text{— if } S_i \cup \{B_i\} \text{ is consistent} \\ S_i & \text{— otherwise} \end{cases}$$

We then put $S_\infty = \cup S_i$. Obviously, S_∞ may depend upon the particular enumeration selected. As McDermott & Doyle point out, if $S = \{MC \rightarrow \sim D, MD \rightarrow \sim C\}$ then, either MC or MD will be selected (but not both) according as C or D is encountered first in the enumeration. To circumvent this problem McDermott & Doyle make their relation of non-monotonic deducibility ($\mathbin{\vdash\!\!\!\sim}$) independent of any particular enumeration by defining

$$S \mathbin{\vdash\!\!\!\sim} A \text{ iff } S_\infty \models A$$

for every enumeration of L_N. As can be easily seen, $\mathbin{\vdash\!\!\!\sim}$ satisfies the so-called rule of possibilitation.

To make this notion of non-monotonic inference a little clearer we examine one example in some detail. Consider the inference

$$\{MC \rightarrow \sim C\} \hspace{0.2em}\vdash\hspace{-0.5em}\sim\hspace{0.3em} A \text{ for any sentence } A \text{ in } L_N.$$

This is sound in the above system. To see this, observe that when C is encountered in any enumeration, MC will be added. At the next stage, however, the condition $MC \in S_i$ and $S_i \models \sim C$ will be satisfied, and S_{i+1} will be the whole language. The non-monotonic behaviour is clearly seen if we 'strengthen' the theory to $\{MC \rightarrow \sim C, C\}$. MC cannot now be derived, and so we will not be able to deduce every sentence in the language.

McDermott points out several rather startling consequences of this theory. First, McDermott proves that non-monotonic $S5$ collapses into monotonic $S5$, that is, if $S \hspace{0.2em}\vdash\hspace{-0.3em}_{S5} A$ then $S \models_{S5} A$. This is rather unfortunate but at least it shows that non-monotonic $S5$ is consistent. The price paid, however, is surely too high, for all the non-montonic reasoning is redundant in this theory. Fortunately, $S4$ and T do not succumb to this collapse. Instead, we have to be concerned about their consistency. Consider the following example due to McDermott. In non-monotonic T (and $S4$) the theory $\{LMC \rightarrow \sim C\}$ is inconsistent, but in T (and $S4$) itself the theory is consistent. This raises doubts about the consistency of non-monotonic T (and $S4$). McDermott actually proves the consistency for the propositional case but, as far as I know, the consistency of the full quantificational regime is still not settled.

Not withstanding all this I believe there is an even more fundamental problem with McDermott's approach. What is the intended interpretation of the operator M in McDermott's semantics? What are the intuitions underlying this modal interpretation? According to the semantic clause, MA is true at a world w, just in case A is true at some world accessible to w. But what are we to intuitively understand by 'accessible' here? I take it that possible worlds are to be understood as complete states of affairs. If so 'accessibility' cannot be understood as 'is consistent with' — at least not under any obvious interpretation of the term 'consistent'. If possible worlds are 'complete states of affairs' no two distinct worlds can be considered 'consistent' in any obvious sense. It really is quite difficult to grasp what intuitions McDermott is appealing to. Perhaps there are not meant to be any, and all of McDermott's semantics is no more than a formal device to define precisely the nature of non-monotonic reasoning. But, if so, this is indefensible. Any semantic theory worthy of its name must capture some underlying intuitions which relate in some way to our primitive understanding of the constructs of the language. It seems that McDermott's approach appears neither to be intuitively sound nor formally satisfactory.

For some more insights into the problems faced by McDermott & Doyle's approach the reader should consult the work of Moore examined in section 5.5.

5.3 INTUITIONISTIC BASIS FOR NON-MONOTONIC LOGIC

The systems of non-monotonic logic due to McDermott & Doyle are based upon a foundation of classical logic. Their basic notion of non-monotonic inference is parasitic upon classical first-order inference. Gabbay (1982) proposes an alternative basis. In Gabbay's system the underlying notion of inference is that of intuitionistic logic.

Gabbay proposes a semantics for L_N (actually just the propositional part) which supports intuitionistic reasoning. To motivate his semantics he requires us to consider situations, typical of non-monotonic reasoning, where we have only a partial knowledge of the actual state of affairs. At any given moment of time we may know that certain statements are true and that certain others are false, but we certainly do not know everything. If we did, there would, presumably, be no need to resort to any form of non-monotonic inference. As time proceeds, however, our knowledge increases. Certain of these undetermined statements are decided one way or the other. It is this setting which seems fundamental to our understanding of Gabbay's semantics.

To capture such intuitions Gabbay employs model structures which involve moments of time and an earlier/later than relation between such.

Definition 3.1 A *Gabbay structure* $T = \langle T, \leqslant \rangle$ where T is a non-empty set (moments of time) and $\leqslant$ is a reflexive and transitive relation on T, that is, for each t, t', t'' in T we have $t \leqslant t$ and ($t \leqslant t'$ & $t' \leqslant t''$ implies $t \leqslant t''$).

Gabbay only supplies the semantics for the propositional part of L_N, and we shall not attempt to extend his theory to the whole language. Since the semantics is to support intuitionistic logic, however, we must admit $\rightarrow$ and v among the primitives of the language. Gabbay actually includes in his model structures a function h which assigns to each atomic wff and moment of time either the value 1 or

0. It is, in addition, subject to the constraint that if $h(t, A) = 1$ and $t' \geqslant t$ then $h(t', A) = 1$. The function h is then extended to all the wffs (of the propositional part of L_N) by recursion as follows:

(i) $h(t, A \& B) = 1$ iff $h(t, A) = 1$ and $h(t, B) = 1$
(ii) $h(t, A \vee B) = 1$ iff $h(t, A) = 1$ or $h(t, B) = 1$
(iii) $h(t, \sim A) = 1$ iff $(\forall s \geqslant t)\,(h(s, A) = 0)$
(iv) $h(t, A \rightarrow B) = 1$ iff $(\forall s \geqslant t)\,(h(s, A) = 1$ implies $h(s, B) = 1)$
(v) $h(t, MA) = 1$ iff $(\exists s \geqslant t)\,(h(s, A) = 1)$.

Some of these clauses require some comment. The analysis of implication derives its impetus from Kripke semantics for intuitionisitic logic. The operator M is interpreted as true of a wff, at a moment in time, if it is true in some possible continuation of that time. Observe that $h(t, \sim A) = 1$ and $h(t, MA) = 1$ are mutually exclusive: $\sim A$ and MA cannot be true at the same moment.

Gabbay defines $A \models B$ (A 'proves' B) iff for any t and h, if $h(t, A) = 1$ then so does $h(t, B)$. The relation of non-monotonic provability will be based upon this notion. Before we turn to this, however, we ought to look more closely at what axioms and rules of inference are supported by this system.

Obviously, such a semantics will not sustain all the classical tautologies. In particular, the law of excluded middle fails. Gabbay lists the following principles which do hold.

(a) $MA \vee \sim A$
(b) $\sim MA \leftrightarrow \sim A$
(c) $(MA \rightarrow B) \leftrightarrow (\sim A \vee B)$
(d) $(MA \rightarrow \sim C) \leftrightarrow \sim C$

As Gabbay points out, the logic of this system is not actually weaker than classical logic; it just affords more opportunities for formulation. As an example of this, Gabbay indicates that for any wff of the propositional calculus:

$$A \vdash \sim B \qquad\qquad \text{iff} \qquad\qquad A \models \sim B$$
$$\text{classically} \qquad\qquad\qquad\qquad \text{intuitionistically}$$

In his criticism of the earlier presentation of McDermott & Doyle, Gabbay cites three problems with their system which he labels as difficulties A, B, and C. (It is worth pointing out that McDermott & Doyle were aware of these problems, and they formed part of the motivation for McDermott's later presentation).

Difficulty A

The rule $\dfrac{\sim MC}{\sim C}$ though intuitively sound is invalid in McDermott & Doyle's early presentation. Their logic was too weak to sanction such an inference. Under Gabbay's system, however, the rule is valid.

Difficulty B

The rule $\dfrac{M(A \;\&\; B)}{MA}$ is again intuitively sound under any interpretation of M as 'plausible' or 'consistent'. It is unsound in the early system of McDermott and Doyle but valid under Gabbay's.

Difficulty C

$\{MC, \sim C\}$ is not inconsistent in McDermott & Doyle's early system, but it is in Gabbay's.

The resolution of these difficulties is a really positive point in favour of Gabbay's presentation. Apparently, though, these difficulties are resolved in McDermott's later presentation.

Gabbay actually presents a complete axiomatisation of his semantics (presumably extended to the whole of L_N), but we shall not include it here.

We are now in a position to define Gabbay's notion of non-monotonic provability. It is more like Reiter's default reasoning than McDermott & Doyle's 'fixed point' rule. Before we provide Gabbay's rule, therefore, it will be instructive to say a little about Reiter's default rule.

Reiter (1980) provides a theory of default reasoning within the context of first-order logic. For Reiter a *default* is any expression of the form

$$A(\overline{x}) : MB_1(\overline{x}), \ldots, MB_m(\overline{x})$$
$$\overline{\rule{5cm}{0.4pt}}$$
$$C(\overline{x})$$

where $A(\overline{x}), B_1(\overline{x}), \ldots, B_m(\overline{x}), C(\overline{x})$ are wff whose free variables are those of $\overline{x} = x_1, \ldots, x_n$. $A(\overline{x})$ is called the *prerequisite* of the default and $C(\overline{x})$ the *consequent*.

An example of default reasoning is the following.

$$BIRD(x) : MFLY(x)$$
$$\overline{\rule{5cm}{0.4pt}}$$
$$FLY(x)$$

We are to interpret this inference as 'If x is a bird and it is consistent to assume that x can fly, then infer that x can fly'. The crucial observation here, of course, is that some birds cannot fly (for example, penguins).

Gabbay's rule of non-monotonic inference is just the transitive closure of Reiter's default rule.

Definition 3.2 We say that B *non-monotonically follows from A* written $A \hspace{1mm} \vdash B$ iff there exists wff $C_0 = A, C_1, \ldots, C_n = B$ and a set of formulae

$$MX_1^1, \ldots, MX_{k\,(1)}^1$$

$$- \qquad -$$

$$- \qquad -$$

$$- \qquad -$$

$$MX_1^n, \ldots, MX_{k\,(n)}^n$$

called the extra assumptions (like defaults) such that for all $1 \leqslant i \leqslant n$, $1 \leqslant j \leqslant k\,(i)$

$$C_i \, \& \, \overset{k\,(i)}{\underset{j=1}{\wedge}} \, MX_j^i \models C_{i+1} \, .$$

Gabbay provides several examples of such non-monotonic inference, but we discuss only one. Suppose $A \, \& \, MB \models C$ and $C \, \& \, MD \models E$. Then using MB as default we can non-monotonically infer C from A. Therefore, $A \hspace{1mm} \vdash C$. On the other hand, using MD as default we can non-monotonically infer E from C. Therefore, $C \hspace{1mm} \vdash E$. Using the transitivity of $\vdash$ (implicit in the definition) we can conclude $A \hspace{1mm} \vdash E$. The reader should consult Gabbay's paper for other examples.

In passing, it is worth mentioning that Gabbay has an alternative system with a different primitive (other than M). There is, however, no explicit semantics provided.

5.4 PARTIAL MODELS AND INCOMPLETE INFORMATION

What seems implicit in Gabbay's proposal is that non-monotonic reasoning is only necessary, and indeed appropriate, in those situations where we have only partial knowledge of the actual state of affairs. Where everything pertinent to the investigation is known, monotonic reasoning suffices. We only need to reason non-monotonically where we are in a state of partial ignorance: some things are known but others are in doubt. If these observations are correct then any attempt to base non-monotonic inference on classical model theory seems intuitively unsound. Instead, any formal semantic theory of such inference should be guided by these intuitions and employ a model theory which facilitates the representation of such 'partial states of information'. There are several ways in which we might proceed in this regard, and Gabbay's proposal represents one, but the development in Chapter 3 offers a second alternative. There we introduced the concept of a partial model for the predicate calculus. It is this notion which will form a central pivot in our theory of non-monotonic inference. For convenience we repeat the main definition.

Definition 4.1 A *partial model* for L (our language of the predicate calculus) is a structure $M = \langle D, F \rangle$ where D is a non-empty set and F is a function which assigns to each n-place relation symbol, C (for each $n > 0$) of L, an n-place function C^M from D^n to $\{t, f, u\}$.

Our incomplete states of knowledge about the world are to be formally represented by such partial models. In essence, they codify our knowledge in terms of the properties ascribed to certain objects and the relations which hold between them. Such models permit us to give a semantics for L (the language of the predicate calculus) which enlists Kleene's strong three-valued connectives.

How precisely are we to deploy such models in our analysis of non-monotonic reasoning? To guide our intuitions here, we shall examine, once again, the airline example due to Dov Gabbay. In their first stab at decision making the Stuttgart office made the following assumption.

(b) Assumed true at 12.00 hours, on the basis of company procedures, and no evidence to the contrary: C = Flight rerouted to London.

Assumption C seemed *plausible* to the Stuttgart office, given their knowledge of company procedures. As things turned out, of course, the assumption was incorrect, but, given the information they had to go on, it seemed a likely contingency. The important point here is that the assumption was not just consistent with what they knew, in some purely extensional sense (for example, in terms of the predicate calculus proof theory, say), but also seemed likely or plausible. In practice we don't just jump to any old conclusion when we don't know the full picture, but rather we follow hunches; we employ our past experience and knowledge to judge which assumptions are plausible or likely and which ones are not. I take it then that any semantic theory of non-monotonic inference must have some under-pinning in which such a notion as 'a plausible assumption' plays a crucial role.

How can this notion be incorporated into the current regime of partial models? What does it mean to assert that a certain assumption is plausible relative to such a partial state of knowledge? Presumably, it will be so if we can imagine a 'plausible extension' to our current state of knowledge, in which the assumption is true, so that our formal notion of 'plausibility' will operate between such partial states of knowledge represented by our partial models. This suggests that we introduce an ordering between such models which intuitively reflects the fact that certain models are 'plausible extensions' to certain others. To this end, let $M \sqsubseteq M'$ signify that M' is a 'plausible extension' of M. Of course, just as in the case of the accessibility relation between possible worlds in modal logic, we cannot spell out exactly what this means. The notion will remain somewhat vague. The best that we can do is to impose properties on this ordering which are dictated by very general intuitions concerning our understanding of the term 'plausible'. Indeed, as regards the logic of the term 'plausible' this is all we require.

Our first observation in this context concerns the notion of 'extension' itself. For one model to be a 'plausible extension' of a second it should, presumably, be an 'extension' of it in some sense. Fortunately, in the current framework of partial models, this term has a very natural exposition. We repeat the definition of Chapter 3.

Definition 4.2 Let M, M' be partial models of L. We shall say M' is an extension of M just in case for each n-place relation, C, of L (each $n > 0$) $C^{M'}$ is an extension of C^{M} (considered as functions from D^n to $\{t, f, u\}$). We write $M \leqslant M'$ to signify that M' is an extension of M.

So one model is an extension of a second if each of its relations is an extension of the corresponding relation in the second. This brings us nicely to our first condition on our notion of plausible extension: if M' is a plausible extension of M, then M' is an extension of M. In other words:

(1) $M \sqsubseteq M'$ implies $M \leqslant M'$.

We cannot, of course, demand that the converse of this implication should hold. To do so would facilitate the collapse of our notion of 'plausible extension' into a purely extensional one; and whatever further constraints we might wish to impose upon this notion, one thing that seems clear is that, like the relation of accessibility between possible worlds, the plausibility ordering on parital models has an 'intensional' character.

Intuitions seem to demand that $\sqsubseteq$ be reflexive and transitive:

(2) $M \sqsubseteq M$

(3) $M \sqsubseteq M'$ and $M' \sqsubseteq M''$ implies $M \sqsubseteq M''$.

Condition (2) seems clear enough; it simply states that every model is a plausible extension of itself. The transitivity axiom also seems intuitively sound — if M' is a plausible extension of M and M'' is a plausible extension of M' then, presumably, M'' is a plausible extension M. We shall call any ordering on partial models of L, which satisfies (1), (2), and (3), a *plausibility ordering*.

We are now in a position to exploit this framework to provide a semantics for McDermott & Doyle's language of non-monotonic logic.

We shall provide the semantics for L_N with respect to the following notion.

Definition 4.3 A *model structure* for L_N is $S = \langle F, \sqsubseteq \rangle$ where F consists of all partial models on a fixed domain of individuals D and $\sqsubseteq$ is a plausibility ordering on F.

In what follows we shall assume that each element, d, of D is named by some constant symbol d' of L_N.

Let S be such a model structure for L_N. We recursively define the truth-conditions for L_N with respect to S by assigning to each *closed* wff a truth-value. We deal first with L itself.

(i) $[C(d'_0, \ldots, d'_{n-1})]^M = C^M(d_0, \ldots, d_{n-1})$

(ii) $[A \& B]^M = [A]^M \wedge [B]^M$

(iii) $[\sim A]^M = \neg[A]^M$

(iv) $[\forall x\, A]^M = \bigwedge_{d \in D} [A(d)]^M$

where $\wedge$, $\neg$, $\bigwedge$ are Kleene's strong connectives. This is exactly the semantics of Chapter 3.

The semantics of the operator M requires more thought. Intuitively, we want MA to be true at a model M just in case there is a plausible extension of M in which A is true and we want it to be false at M if and only if it is false in all plausible extensions. This leads to:

(v) $[MA]^M = \bigvee_{M' \in P_M} [A]^{M'}$

where $P_M = \{M' \in F : M \sqsubseteq M'\}$
and

$$\bigvee_{i \in I} f_i = \begin{cases} 1 & \text{if some } f_i = 1 \\ 0 & \text{if each } f_i = 0 \\ u & \text{otherwise.} \end{cases}$$

The following result of Chapter 3 is important in as much as it illustrates the monotonic character of L, which is to be seen in contrast to the non-monotonic character of L_N itself.

Theorem 4.4 (Monotonicity) For each $A \in L$, if $M \leqslant M'$, then $[A]^M \leqslant [A]^{M'}$

This monotonicity condition does not extend to the whole of L_N. The operator M is essentially non-monotonic. This seems intuitively right: because MA is plausible from the perspective of M then we ought not to demand that it be plausible in all extensions. The whole framework is much less well-behaved.

This completes our basic framework for the investigation of non-monotonic inference. It obviously has much in common with Gabby's proposal, but where the latter employs a base of intuitionistic logic the present theory employs Kleenes' strong three-valued logic.

How does our semantics fare with respect to the difficulties A, B and C cited by Gabbay? To investigate this we require a preliminary definition. We shall say that B follows from A, if for each model structure S and partial model M of S if $[A]^M = 1$ then $[B]^M = 1$. We write this as $A \models B$.

It is quite easy to see that inference rule (A) is valid: if $[MA]^M = 0$ then for each $M' \sqsubseteq M$, $[A]^{M'} = 0$. By the reflexive axiom for $\sqsubseteq$, $M \sqsubseteq M$ and so $[A]^M = 0$, as required. Furthermore, inference rule (B) is valid: if $[M(A \& B)]^M = 1$ then for some $M' \sqsubseteq M$, $[A \& B]^{M'} = 1$ and hence $[A]^{M'} = 1$. Difficulty C is a little more troublesome. $\{MA, \sim A\}$ is indeed inconsistent when A is restricted to L (that is, involves no occurrences of the operator M). To see this observe that if $[MA]^M = 1$ and $[A]^M = $ then, since $A \in L$, $[A]^M = 0$ implies $[A]^{M'} = 0$ for each $M' \sqsubseteq M$ (by monotonicity). But this contradicts $[MA]^M = 1$. This seems intuitively correct. Those intuitions which demand that $\{MA, \sim A\}$ be inconsistent rely crucially on the monotonic behaviour of A. Where A is permitted to change its truth-value in extensions of our knowledge there is no intuitive reason to demand the inconsistency of $\{MA, \sim A\}$.

In this section we are only advocating an alternative *basis* for non-monotonic inference. We believe that our proposal is closely allied to the mechanisms we employ in reasoning with incomplete information. As regards the rule of non-monotonic inference we could either employ the fixed-point rule of McDermott & Doyle or the default mechanism of Reiter and Gabbay, but like Gabbay we prefer the latter. We believe that the system outlined here is worthy of further investigation.

5.5 AUTOEPISTEMIC LOGIC

In a recent paper, Bob Moore (Moore 1983) offers a intriguing contribution to the non-monotonic logic literature. Moore distinguishes between 'default reasoning' and 'autoepistemic reasoning'. By default reasoning he understands the process of drawing inferences, from less than conclusive evidence, in the absence of any information to the contrary. It is characteristic of such reasoning that its conclusions are tentative: they may well be withdrawn in the light of new information. Autoepistemic reasoning is said not to be of this genre. It involves reasoning about one's own belief or knowledge. It is intended to model the reasoning of an ideally rational agent reflecting upon his beliefs.

Autoepistemic logic takes sets of sentences or theories as the primary objects of study where these sentences are selected from the propositional part of L_N. Such a theory is meant to represent the total beliefs of an agent, and Moore dignifies them with the name *autoepistemic theories*. In such an administration the modal operator L is to be interpreted as 'is believed'. His theory centres upon the following semantic notions

Definition 5.1 A *Propositional interpretation* of an autoepistemic theory T is an assignment, f, of truth-values $(1, 0)$ to L_N such that

$$f(A \ \& \ B) = 1 \quad \text{iff} \quad f(A) = 1 \text{ and } f(B) = 1$$
$$f(\sim A) \quad = 1 \quad \text{iff} \quad f(A) = 0$$

A *propositional model* (or model) of an autoepistemic theory T is a propositional interpretation of T in which every sentence of T is assigned the value 1.

An *autoepistemic interpretation* of an autoepistemic theory T is a propositional interpretation, f, of T which satisfies $f(LA) = 1$ iff $A \in T$ for every sentence A.

An *autoepistemic model* of an autoepistemic theory T is an autoepistemic interpretation in which every sentence of T is assigned the value 1.

As Moore puts it, autoepistemic interpretations and models of a theory T are exactly those interpretations and models that conform to the intended meaning of the modal operator L.

Moore insists on two constraints that must be imposed on any notion of inference pertaining to autoepistemic logic. The intuitions here relate to the question of what beliefs an ideally rational agent ought to adopt on the basis of certain initial premises. The belief sets of such agents ought to be both 'sound' and 'complete'. Such a set of beliefs is *sound,* with respect to a set of premises, if the beliefs are true if the premises are; it is *complete* if it contains every sentence that the agent is semantically justified in concluding from the assumption that his beliefs are true (and the knowledge that they are his beliefs). These ideas are expressed formally as follows.

Definition 5.2 An autoepistemic theory, T, is *sound,* with respect to a set of premises S, iff every autoepistemic interpretation of T, which is a propositional model of S, is a model of T.

An autoepistemic theory T is *semantically complete* iff T contains every sentence that is true in every autoepistemic model of T.

Moore next addresses the question of providing a proof-theoretic or syntactic characterisation of those autoepistemic theories which satisfy the constraints of soundness and completeness.

An autoepistemic theory T, which represents the beliefs of an ideally rational agent, should, according to Moore, satisfy the following constraints:

    I   If $A1, \ldots, An$ are in T and $A1, \ldots, An \vdash B$ (where $\vdash$ is tautological consequence) then B is in T.

    II If A is in T, then LA is in T.

    III If A is not in T, then $\sim LA$ is in T.

Theories which satisfy I, II and III are called *stable.* These coincide with the complete theories.

Theorem 5.2 An autoepistemic theory is semantically complete iff it is stable.

Corresponding to soundness, Moore introduces the syntactic notion of *groundedness.* An autoepistemic theory is *grounded,* in a set of premises S, iff every sentence of S is included in the tautological consequences of $S \cup \{LA : A \in T\} \cup \{\sim LA : A \notin T\}$.

Theorem 5.4 An autoepistemic theory T is sound, with respect to an initial set of premises S, iff T is grounded in S.

Moore's theory provides some insight into the peculiarities of McDermott & Doyle's theory of non-monotonic inference. McDermott & Doyle's first logic is very similar to autoepistemic logic, but there is a major difference. McDermott & Doyle have nothing in their logic corresponding to Moore's condition (II) (if A is in T, then LA is in T). In a stable theory, T, if A is in T then so is LA. This is false in

McDermott & Doyle's fixed-point theories. This seems to explain quite nicely the peculiarities of McDermott & Doyle's original logic. For example, the fact that MC does not follow from M(C & D) (or equivalently $\sim L C$ does not follow from $\sim$L(C v D)) is nicely explained. Since their logic lacks the facility to infer LA from A it admits of interpretations more restricted than Moore's.

Moore's theory also provides an explanation of the curiosities of McDermott's modal theory of non-monotonic inference. Changing the base logic to a modal logic brings the theory closer to auto-epistemic logic. Adding $A \vdash$ LA as an inference rule certainly strengthens the logic, but Moore claims that it does this in the wrong way. In Moore's theory {LA : $A \in T$} is added to the base of T; in McDermott's theory $A \vdash$ LA is added as a new rule of inference. As a consequence not all stable expansions of a theory S are fixed points of S. In autoepistemic logic LA has to be true to be in the belief set of an agent, whereas in McDermott's logic it must be grounded in a derivation of A that does not rely upon LA.

I believe that Moore's theory is an interesting one and is certainly worthy of further study and investigation. In particular, the advantages and disadvantages of autoepistemic logic over the other theories developed in this chapter provide much food for thought. It seems that the theories developed in sections 3 and 4 of this chapter should be classified as default theories under Moore's criterion, and so perhaps they ought not to be viewed as rivals to autoepistemic logic.

BIBLIOGRAPHICAL NOTES

Reiter's paper contains an alternative approach to that of McDermott & Doyle. In Reiter's theory non-monotonic rules are to be conceptu-alised as rules which permit theory extensions. Gabbay's rule of non-monotonic inference is based upon Reiter's proposal. McCarthy (1980) attempts to capture an idea inherent in Occam's razor: one should only assume the existence of those objects which are minimally required by the contexts. Davis (1980) contains some insightful technical observations concerning McCarthy's notion of circumscrip-tion. The recent proceedings of the Eighth International Joint Conference on AI contain several recent contributions to the subject. The standard of papers is rather mixed, but most are worthy of a brief read.

Davis, M. (1980) 'The mathematics of non-monotonic reasoning' in: *Artificial Intelligence* 13 73–80.

Doyle, J. (1982) 'A truth maintenance system' in: *Artificial Intelligence* 12 231–272.

Doyle, J. (1983) 'The ins and outs of reason maintenance' in: *Proc. 8th Int. Joint Conf. on Artificial Intelligence (1983)* 349–351.

Gabbay, D. (1982) 'Intuitionistic basis for non-monotonic logic' in: *Proc. Conf. on Automated Deduction,* Springer Lecture Notes in Computer Science, No. 6, 260–273.

Hewitt, C. E. (1971) IJCAI 1971.

Hewitt, C. E. (1973) 'Description and theoretical analysis of PLANNER: a language for proving theorems and manipulating a robot', Massachusetts Institute of Technology, A.I. Laboratory, *Report TR–258.*

Lukaszewisz, W. (1983) 'General approach to non-monotonic logics' in: *Proc. 8th Int. Joint Conf. on Artificial Intelligence (1983),* Karlsruhe 352–354.

McCarthy, J. (1980) 'Circumscription: a form of non-monotonic reasoning' in *Artificial Intelligence* 13 27–39.

McDermott, D. & Doyle, J. (1980) 'Non-monotonic logic I' in: *Artificial Intelligence* 13 27–39.

McDermott, D. (1982) 'Non-monotonic logic II: non-monotonic modal theories' in *JACM* 29 (1) 33–57.

Moore, R. (1983) 'Semantical considerations on nonmonotonic logic', in: *Proc. 8th Int. Joint Conf. on Artificial Intelligence (1983),* 272–279.

Reiter, R. (1980) 'A logic for default reasoning' in: *Aritificial Intelligence* 13 81–132.

Sanderwell, E. (1972) 'An approach to the frame problem, and its implementation' in: Meltzer, B. & Michie, D. (eds), *Machine Intelligence 7,* Edinburgh University Press.

6

Temporal logic in artificial intelligence

6.1 INTRODUCTION

Standard logic, in the form of the predicate calculus, seems ill-equipped to cope with statements containing tensed verbs or explicit temporal reference. For example, in standard logic the assertion 'Socrates is sitting' (where the 'is' means 'is now') has to be rendered as something of the form 'All moments-identical-with-the-present are (timelessly) moments-when-Socrates-is-seated'. Such reformulations are at best awkward and at worst misleading. Moreover, the impoverished expressive ability of standard logic can lead to the marking of certain intuitively sound inferences as invalid. For instance, the following inference

John is running
_____

John will have run

seems intuitively sound but cannot be directly formulated as a valid inference in standard logic.

There are three possible responses to the problem raised by such inferences. Quine (1960), for example, advoctates that such tensed statements should be paraphrased into an atemporal form and represented in a many-sorted predicate calculus. Strawson, on the other hand, sees the above phenomenon as but an indication of the inherent limitations of formal logic. A third response is more positive and advocates an extension of formal logic which can cope with such inferences. Such is the approach of temporal logic. The objective of temporal logic is to elucidate reasoning with statements which have some temporal aspect.

In the next section we shall provide an account of classical temporal logics, but first we say a little about the role of such issues in artificial intelligence.

Until quite recently, temporal considerations have been given scant attention in the AI literature. The common justification is that such considerations would lead to enormous complexities without much compensatory practical gain. Such authors seem to believe that temporal aspects could be added to their systems without any conceptually significant changes. But a close examination of the literature certainly does not support such a view. On the contrary, many authors have to introduce additional complexity in order to avoid any explicit representation of time. For example, in MOLGEN each object is equipped with several names: one for each state in which it exists. Other systems have attempted to compensate for the lack of any explicit representation of time by employing the system's own internal time. As McDermott (1982) points out, this leads to confusion between mistaken beliefs (things believed which were just wrong) and those which are simply no longer true. The ERASE mechanism in PLANNER is a case in point. This served two purposes: eliminating both mistaken hypotheses and assertions no longer true. Clearly these two issues are conceptually quite distinct, and efforts to identify them have led not only to conceptual confusions but also to awkward and inextensible programs.

There are several other, perhaps more positive, considerations which lead one to believe that some representation of time is essential. In medical diagnosis there is a clear need for a representation of 'events' and 'couse-of-events'. One needs to be able to adequately represent not only the course of a disease but also to pinpoint the symptoms characteristic of its various stages. Programs developed for story understanding need to have a representation of the past, whereas planning programs require a way of representing possible furtures.

McDermott (1982) illustrates this latter point in a quite graphic way by reference to a rather amusing example. A problem solver (called Dudley) is confronted with the classic situation of a heroine (call Nell) tied to the tracks with a train rapidly approaching. Dudley knows that

'If Nell is going to be mashed, I must remove her from the tracks.'

Dudley constructs a plan of action. He locates Nell and plots a route to her location. The plan and the intention to carry it out are added to Dudley's data base. Meanwhile, a consistency maintainer (called Harvey) observes that Dudley's intention is to implement the plan and concludes that Nell will no longer be mashed. Subsequently, Harvey removes the intention from Dudley's data base. Unfortunately, there is now no longer any need for the plan, and so Harvey removes that as well. But this means that 'Nell is going to be mashed' is true again, and the whole process repeats itself. Without an explicit representation of time Nell is doomed to be mashed, Dudley bereaved, and Harvey will have no conception of what he has done.

In conclusion, it seems pretty clear that, if AI is to achieve its stated goals, it must incorporate a representation of time and employ some form of temporal logic. The question is, which form is appropriate? It is, perhaps, too early in the development of the subject to answer or even address this question in a useful way. There is certainly no consensus to be found in the literature. Instead, to begin with at least, we shall merely map out the various temporal logics which have been developed by tense logicians.

6.2 TEMPORAL LOGIC

In temporal logic, unlike classical logic, the same sentence may have a different truth-value at different times: a sentence true at some time in the past may not be true now, and a sentence true now may not remain so in the future. It is this phenomenon which provides the characteristic flavour of temporal inference.

We shall restrict our attention to propositional temporal logic, so that our language, L_T is generated from certain atomic sentences by the connectives of the propositional calculus plus the temporal operators F, P, G and H. In other words, L_T is the extension of the language of the propositional calculus which admits sentences of the form FA, PA, GA, HA for any sentence A. The intuitive readings of these operators can be stated as follows:

  (i) FA — A is true at some future time
 (ii) PA — A was true at some past time
(iii) GA — A will be true at all future times
 (iv) HA — A has always been true in the past

In order to take account of this variation of truth-values over time, our basic model-theoretical structures must include some notion of 'points in time' and some relation of temporal precedence.

Definition 2.1 A *temporal frame* T consists of a non-empty set, T, of time points, a relation, R, of temporal precedence, together with a function $h : T \times$ Atomic Sentences of $L_T \rightarrow \{1, 0\}$.

The function h assigns to each atomic sentence its truth-values throughout time. The semantics for the whole of L_T is conveyed by extending the function h to the whole language in the following way.

(i) $h(t, A \& B) = 1$ iff $h(t, A) = 1$ and $h(t, B) = 1$

(ii) $h(t, \sim A) \quad = 1$ iff $h(t, A) = 0$

(iii) $h(t, FA) \quad = 1$ iff $(\exists t')\, (R(t, t') \& h(t', A) = 1)$

(iv) $h(t, PA) \quad = 1$ iff $(\exists t')\, (R(t', t) \& h(t', A) = 1)$

Clauses (iii) and (iv) reflect our intuitive readings of FA and PA, where $R(t, t')$ is understood as expressing the temporal precedence of t over t'. The meanings of GA and HA can be gleaned from the definitions

$$GA \leftrightarrow \sim F \sim A$$
$$HA \leftrightarrow \sim P \sim A$$

So that

$$h(t, GA) \quad = 1 \quad \text{iff} \quad (\forall t')\, (R(t, t') \rightarrow h(t', A) = 1)$$
$$h(t, HA) \quad = 1 \quad \text{iff} \quad (\forall t')\, (R(t', t) \rightarrow h(t', A) = 1)$$

We shall say that a sentence is *true* in such a frame if it takes the value 1 at every point in time.

This account of L_T will remain constant throughout this chapter. The only variation concerns the properties ascribed to the relation of temporal precedence. We obtain different logics by varying the properties ascribed to R.

Minimal temporal logic, K, is obtained by imposing no restrictions on the relation R. We shall say a sentence is *K-valid* iff it is true in all temporal frames. Minimal temporal logic is precisely the set of K-valid sentences and is characterised by the following axiom schemata, (A1–A7), together with *modus ponens* (MP) as the rule of inference.

(A1) A, where A is a tautology

(A2) $G(A \rightarrow B) \rightarrow (GA \rightarrow GB)$

(A3) $H(A \rightarrow B) \rightarrow (HA \rightarrow HB)$

(A4) $A \rightarrow HFA$

(A5) $A \rightarrow GPA$

(A6) GA, if A is an axiom

(A7) HA, if A is an axiom

(MP) If A and $A \rightarrow B$, then B.

The proof that the theorems of this system are precisely the K-valid sentences (the completeness result) can be found in McArthur (1976) or Rescher & Urquhart (1971).

All the other systems of temporal logic that we shall consider are extensions of minimal temporal logic, and are obtained by imposing further constraints on our relation of temporal precedence.

The conception of 'branching time' is obtained by imposing two constraints on R:

(R1) $(\forall t \, \forall s \, \forall r) \, ((R \, (t, s) \, \& \, R \, (s, r) \to R \, (t, r))$
(R2) $(\forall t \, \forall s \, \forall r) \, (R \, (t, r) \, \& \, R \, (s, r) \to R \, (t, s) \vee t = s \vee R \, (s, t))$

Transitivity, (R1), needs little justification and is implicit in any notion of temporal precedence that we might entertain. Condition (R2), referred to as *backwards linearity*, rules out brances in temporal succession of the following form.

Branching time thus insists on there being only one past but permits the future to remain open.

To axiomatise this logic (the sentences true in all frames which satisfy (R1) and (R2)) we need to add two additional schemata to A1–A7.

(A8) $FFA \to FA$
(A9) $(PA \, \& \, PB) \to (P \, (A \, \& \, B) \vee (P(A \, \& \, PB) \vee P \, (PA \, \& \, B)))$

(A8) corresponds to transitivity and (A9) to backwards linearity. Rescher & Urquhart have dubbed this logic K_b.

The classical picture of time is that of a linear series. Such a conception is assumed in a great portion of physics. For example, the absolute time of Newtonian physics is a one-dimensional linear continuum, and even in relativistic physics the ordering of 'local' time series is linear. To capture this conception of time we must strengthen (R2) to rule out branching in the future as well as branching in the past. This is achieved by insisting that R be connected:

(R3) $(\forall s \, \forall t) \, (R \, (s, t) \vee s = t \vee R \, (t, s))$

Obviously, (R3) is equivalent to the conjunction of (R2), and forwards linearity given as:

(R4) $(\forall s \, \forall t \, \forall r) \, (R \, (r, \, t) \, \& \, R(r, \, s) \rightarrow R \, (s, \, t) \vee s = t \vee R \, (t, \, s))$

To characterise the sentences true in all frames which satisfy (R1) and (R3), we need to add to A1–A9 the following schemata:

(A10) $(FA \, \& \, FB) \rightarrow (F \, (A \, \& \, B) \vee (F \, (A \, \& \, FB) \vee F \, (FA \, \& \, B)))$

which corresponds to forwards linearity. The temporal logic defined by A1–A10 (K_1) was introduced by Nino Cocchiarella.

This logic still leaves unanswered many fundamental questions concerning the nature of time. Is there both a first and last moment of time? Is there a moment between any two moments? Is time continuous like the real numbers? Different answers to these questions lead to different temporal logics.

A positive answer to the first question leads to two further constraints on our relation of temporal precedence.

(R5) $(\forall s) \, (\exists t) \, (R \, (t, \, s))$
(R6) $(\forall s) \, (\exists t) \, (R \, (s, \, t))$

(R5) guarantees that time has no beginning, and (R6) that time has no end. The tense logic corresponding to this extension of K_1 is due to Dana Scott, and we shall refer to it as K_s. Its axiomatisation is obtained from the addition of (A11) and (A12) to the schemata of K_1.

(A11) $GA \rightarrow FA$
(A12) $HA \rightarrow PA$

Is there a moment between any two moments? A positive answer leads to a view of time in which the time line has the structure of the rational numbers; a negative answer forces time only to have the structure of the natural numbers. Equivalently, a positive answer forces the time line to be 'dense' in the following sense:

(R7) $(\forall s) \, (\forall t) \, (\exists r) \, (R \, (s, \, t) \rightarrow (R \, (s, \, r) \, \& \, R \, (r, \, t)))$

A. N. Prior is credited with the formulation of dense, linear temporal logic (K_p). It requires one further axiom schemata in addition to those of K_s.

(A13) $FA \rightarrow FFA$

Our last question concerns the issue of whether time is to be just dense, like the rationals, or actually continuous, like the reals. If we divide a densely ordered linear series T into two non-empty sets $T1$ and $T2$, so that every point in $T1$ precedes those in $T2$, three possibilities can arise:

(i) $T1$ has a last member, but $T2$ no first
(ii) $T1$ has no last member, but $T2$ has a first
(iii) $T1$ has no last member and $T2$ no first

The ordering of T is *continuous* if only (i) and (ii) are permitted. This constraint can be expressed as follows:

(R8) $(\forall T1, T2)\,((T = T1 \cup T2\ \&\ (\forall s \in T1)\,(\forall t \in T2)\,(R\,(s,\,t)))$
$$\rightarrow$$
$$(\exists s')\,((\forall s \in T1)\,(R\,(s,\,s')\ \&\ (\forall t \in T2)\,(R\,(s',\,t))))))$$

A little reflection should convince the reader that this rules out possibility (iii).

The above property of the full linear continuum is reflected in the axiom schemata:

(A14) $\square\,(GA \rightarrow PGA) \rightarrow (GA \rightarrow HA)$

where for any sentence B, $\square\,B$ is defined as $GB\ \&\ HB\ \&\ B$. For completeness, we call this logic K_c.

This completes our basic discussion of temporal logic. We now turn our attention to the role of temporal reasoning in AI.

6.3 TWO CASE STUDIES

Generally speaking, there has been very little discussion of temporal considerations in the AI literature. This omission has been rectified to some extent by several recent contributions. In this section we shall discuss two of the more influential of these and attempt to place them within the general framework, of the temporal logics discussed in the previous section.

(i) McDermott's temporal logic

McDermott (1982) employs a temporal logic in which the relation of temporal precedence is transitive, left-linear, infinite in both directions, dense, and continuous. He employs a many-sorted first-order predicate logic with variables permitted to range over a basic ontology of 'times', 'states', 'facts', and 'events'.

'States' are to be thought of, intuitively, as instantaneous snapshots of universe. Attached to each state is a 'date' which is the time at which the universe is (possibly) in that state. Moreover, the set of states is partially ordered by an ordering, $\leqslant$, which is compatible with that of temporal precedence. States are arranged into 'chronicles' where a 'chronicle' is a complete possible history of the universe – a totally ordered set of states which extends infinitely in time. Intuitively, a chronicle is the way events might go, and, according to McDermott, things might go in more than one way.

The significance of states and chronicles arises from the insistence, by McDermott, that they form the stage where 'facts' and 'events' are acted out. 'Facts' are permitted to change their truth-value over time. This curiosity facilitates the identification of facts with sets of states: intuitively, a fact is to be thought of as that set of states in which it is true. For example, (ON A B) apparently denotes a fact, namely that set of states in which A is actually on B.

'Events', according to McDermott, are more difficult to handle than mere facts. They are identified with sets of intervals: those intervals over which the event happens once, with no time left over on either side.

Much of McDermott's paper is given over to an axiomatic characterisation of these notions. To give the reader the flavour of this characterisation we state some of his axioms and definitions. For some obscure reason, McDermott states his axioms in 'Cambridge Polish'. We shall employ the more familiar notation of the predicate calculus.

The partial order, $\leqslant$, between states is taken to be dense,

$$(\forall s1, s2)\ (s1 < s2 \rightarrow (\exists s)\ (s1 < s < s2)),$$

and compatible with that of temporal precedence

$$(\forall s1, s2)\ (s1 < s2 \rightarrow R\ (\text{date}\,(s1),\ \text{date}\,(s2))),$$

where 'date' is a function which assigns to each state its date. Chronicles are totally ordered sets of states:

$$\text{Chronicle}\ (x) = \text{def}\quad (\forall y)\ (y \in x \rightarrow \text{state}\,(y))\ \&$$
$$(\forall s1, s2)\ (s1 \in x\ \&\ s2 \in x)\ (s1 < s2 \vee s1 =$$
$$s2 \vee s2 < s1)\ \&$$
$$(\forall t)\ (\exists s)\ (s \in x\ \&\ \text{date}\,(s) = t)$$

The relation between states, times, and chronicles is best summarised as follows:

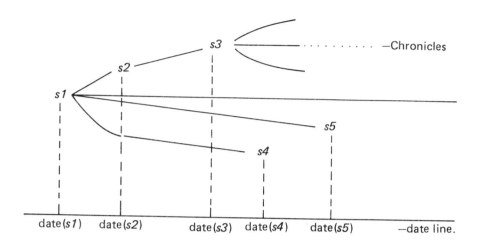

McDermott's enterprise is ambitious. His temporal logic enables one to prove results about facts, events, and plans, and world histories. In particular, the logic facilitates an analysis of causality, continuous change in quantities, the frame problem, and the relationship between tasks and actions. If this were not enough, he goes on to sketch an implementation of a 'temporal inference machine' based upon his logic.

Despite the length and amount of detail in the paper, I have certain reservations about this type of approach to the problems addressed. The paper meanders through some of the most treacherous terrain in philosophical logic. Very little attention is given to the host of technical and philosophical concerns which pervade the subject. The account of events seems particularly problematic. Why should an event be identified with a set of intervals? Whatever notion of event we might entertain, this identification just seems wrong. The two notions seem entirely different. Sets of intervals are sets of sets of instants, on McDermott's account, and surely if we can talk about durationless instants at all, such talk must arise from the intuitions relating to the events themselves and the temporal relations by which they are connected. Furthermore, the blending of object and metalanguage, together with the considerable number of axioms employed (44 in all) leave one with doubts about the theory's consistency. I have no doubt that AI programs must employ temporal knowledge if AI is to achieve its stated goals, but surely one must pay some attention to the philosophical and technical foundations of the subject.

(ii) Allen's temporal logic

Allen (1981) is also an attempt to incorporate temporal reasoning into AI programs. Allen is concerned with formalising the types of knowledge required to reason about actions and events. Like McDermott, he employs a many-sorted predicate calculus with variables ranging over 'properties', 'time intervals', 'events', and much else besides.

The account of time he offers is somewhat different from standard accounts in that intervals, and temporal relations between them, are taken as primitive. The temporal relations between intervals are the following:

(i)   During ($i1$, $i2$)   —   time interval $i1$ is fully contained within $i2$, although they may coincide on their end points;

(ii) Before ($i1$, $i2$)   —   time interval $i1$ is before $i2$, and they do not overlap;

(iii) Overlap ($i1$, $i2$) —   interval $i1$ starts before $i2$, and they overlap;

(iv) Meets ($i1$, $i2$)   —   interval $i1$ is before $i2$, but there is no interval between them, that is, $i1$ ends where $i2$ starts;

(v)   Equal ($i1$, $i2$)   — $i1$ and $i2$ are the same interval.

Each of these relations is represented by a predicate in the logic, and they are governed by a set of axioms of which the following are representative:

(T1)   Before ($i1$, $i2$) & Before ($i2$, $i3$) → Before ($i1$, $i3$)

(T2)   Meets ($i1$, $i2$) & During ($i2$, $i3$) → (Overlaps ($i1$, $i3$) v During ($i1$, $i3$) v Meets ($i1$, $i3$))

(T3)   Overlaps ($i1$, $i2$) → ($\exists i$) (During (i, $i1$) & During (i, $i2$))

(T4)   Meets ($i1$, $i2$) → $\sim$($\exists i$) (Before ($i1$, i) & Before (i, $i2$))

(T5)   Meets ($i1$, $i2$) v Before ($i1$, $i2$) → $\sim$($\exists i$) (During (i, $i1$) & During (i, $i2$))

All of these can be justified by thinking of the intervals as constructed from a system in which time points are primitive, but Allen takes intervals as primitive to emphasise the importance of 'interval based reasoning' in AI applications. However, Allen does introduce a notion of instant or point axiomatically. He introduces the predicate 'Point' where intuitively Point (i) is to signify that i is a 'very small' interval. Point intervals are not permitted to overlap or contain other intervals etc.

(T6)   Point (i) → ~ Overlap $(i, i1)$ & ~ Overlap $(i1, i)$
(T7)   Point $(i1)$ & Point $(i2)$ → ~Meet $(i1, i2)$
(T8)   Point (i) → ~During $(i1, i)$

Properties are said to hold at intervals, and Allen introduces the predicate

Holds (p, i)

to indicate that the property p holds at interval i. To allow properties to name complex logical expressions Allen introduces functions 'and', 'or', 'not', 'all', and 'exists' which correspond to the familiar logical operators in the following way:

(H1)   Holds (and $(p, q), i)$ ↔ Holds (p, i) & Holds (q, i)
(H2)   Holds (or $(p, q), i)$ ↔ $(\forall i1)$(Point $(i1)$ & During $(i1, i)$ →
          Holds $(p, i1)$ v Holds $(q, i1)$)
(H3)   Holds (not $(p), i)$ → ~Holds(p, i))
(H4)   Point (i) → (Holds (not $(p), i)$ ↔ ~ Holds (p, i))
(H5)   Holds (all $(x, p), i)$ ↔ $\forall x$ Holds (p, i)
(H6)   Holds (exists $(x, p), i)$ ↔ $(\forall i1)$ (Point $(i1)$ & During $(i1, i)$ →
          $\exists x$ Holds $(p, i1)$)

Notice how the accounts of disjunction and conjunction (and existential and universal quantification) are very different. Why should this be? Allen offers little or no justification for this seemingly arbitrary decision.

'Events' are introduced as a new primitive in the logic. Allen introduces a predicate 'Change-pos' which takes four arguments: the object, the source, the goal location, and the move itself. For example,

Change-Pos (Ball, x, y, e)

asserts that e is an event consisting of the ball moving from x to y. We are able to assert that this event occurred over time interval i by the assertion

Occur (e, i)

and this enables Allen to state necessary and sufficient conditions for the event's occurrence:

Change-pos (object, source, goal, e) & Occur (e, i)
↔
$(\exists i1, i2)$ (Meets $(i1, i)$ & Meets $(i, i2)$ &
          Holds (at (object, source), $i1$) &
          Holds (at (object, goal), $i2$)
)

Allen goes on to describe 'actions' as a particular type of event, namely those which are caused by agents.

I prefer the account of Allen's to that of McDermott if only because events are taken as primitive (which seems intuitively sound) and 'chunks of time' are utilised instead of instants. I believe, however, that additional clarification is needed as to the relationship between intervals, points, and events. As we have stated before, our intuitions concerning instants (and intervals) seem to be parasitic upon those intuitions relating to the events themselves and the temporal relations by which they are connected. Nothing of this intimate relationship is brought out by Allen's account except in so far as the predicate 'Occur' is introduced into the language of the logic. Nor is it very clear what a semantics for Allen's language would look like. He has obviously defined a first-order theory of some description, but what form do models of this theory take? In particular, with his axiomatisation of intervals, do points really correspond to maximally overlapping sets of intervals?

Allen's account also employs a considerable number of axioms, and so my criticisms of McDermott's paper, regarding consistency, seem to apply here as well. Neither of these authors utilises temporal logics exactly in the form in which they are presented in section 6.2. They certainly employ the notions of temporal frame (implicitly) but not the language of temporal logic. Instead, their languages permit explicit reference to times and intervals: they employ the metalanaguage of temporal logic. Their approach has more in common with that advocated by Quine than that advanced by temporal logicians. This seems largely to be an artefact of their concern with actions, events, and planning. Very little attention seems to have been paid to the actual mechanisms in natural language which facilitate temporal reference. Indeed, McDermott seems to suggest that such considerations are irrelevant to the AI enterprise. This seems too strong a claim. The more sophisticated studies of tense and aspect in natural language recently undertaken by linguistics and tense logicians are surely relevant to the AI enterprise. Certainly the papers of Kamp(1979, 1980) are worthy of further consideration.

6.4 EVENTS AND INSTANTS

In my opinion, one of the central conceptual problems in the application of standard temporal logic to AI concerns the interplay between events and time. McDermott, for example, employs a representation where events are defined in terms of instants. Allen, on the other hand, takes both events and intervals as primitive, and events are said to occur over intervals of time. Neither author offers much by way of clarification regarding the exact relationship between the two.

One observation, which does seem right, is that events ought to be taken as conceptually prior to instants, and this seems so whether or not we regard events as some sort of mental experience or physical phenomenon. Indeed, if we are able to talk about durationless instants at all, such talk must ultimately be unpacked in terms of those intuitions which relate directly to events and their temporal relationship. In this section we develop such an account of time. The construction that we shall employ is due to Wiener (1914) and has been recently resurrected in Temporal logic by Kamp (1978, 1980) and Van Benthem (1983). The construction provides us with instants, at each of which the event is going on. Before we proceed with the construction, however, we need to spell out the structural properties of the events themselves.

These properties are given in terms of two temporal relations between events: the relation of temporal overlap and that of temporal precedence.

Definition 4.1 An *event structure* $E = \langle E, \sqsubset, 0 \rangle$ consists of a non-empty set E of events together with two binary relations, $\sqsubset$, of temporal precedence and, 0, of temporal overlap, which satisfy (E1)–(E7) below.

(E1) $e_1 \sqsubset e_2 \rightarrow \sim (e_2 \, 0 \, e_1)$;
(E2) $e_1 \sqsubset e_2 \, \& \, e_2 \sqsubset e_3 \rightarrow e_1 \sqsubset e_3$;
(E3) $e_1 \, 0 \, e_2 \rightarrow e_2 \, 0 \, e_1$;
(E4) $e_1 \, 0 \, e_1$;
(E5) $e_1 \sqsubset e_2 \rightarrow \sim (e_1 \, 0 \, e_2)$
(E6) $e_1 \sqsubset e_2 \, \& \, e_2 \, 0 \, e_3 \, \& \, e_3 \sqsubset e_4 \rightarrow e_1 \sqsubset e_4$;
(E7) $e_1 \sqsubset e_2 \, \vee \, e_1 \, 0 \, e_2 \, \vee \, e_2 \sqsubset e_1$.

Postulates (E1)–(E6) are intuitively sound, given any notions of temporal overlap and precedence between events that we might entertain. Kamp (1980) objects to (E7), however, on the grounds that it is not always possible to delineate events precisely enough to say, of any two events, that one of the contingencies enumerated in (E7) holds. Kamp subsequently develops a much more elaborate theory. We shall not follow suit here since our aim is merely to present the elementary portions of this developing approach to temporal logic.

This brings us to the construction itself. Roughly, instants are to be recovered from such a structure as maximal subsets of pairwise overlapping events.

Definition 4.2 Let E be an event structure. An *Instant* i is a subset of E such that:

(i) $(\forall e_1, e_2 \in i)\,(e_1 \; 0 \; e_2)$
(ii) $(\forall e_1 \in E - i)\,(\exists e_2 \in i)\,(\sim e_1 \; 0 \; e_2)$
Let $I(E)$ be the set of instants of E.

The ordering of temporal precedence on instants is defined in terms of that on events as follows. Let $i_1, i_2 \in I(E)$, then define

$$i_1 <_E i_2 =_{\text{def}} (\exists e_1 \in i_1)\,(\exists e_2 \in i_2)\,(e_1 \sqsubset e_2)$$

Let $T_E = \langle I(E), <_E \rangle$.

Theorem 4.3 Let E be an event structure. Then T_E is a strict linear ordering
Proof We must show that $<_E$ (written $<$) satisfies the following conditions

(i) $i_1 < i_2 \to \sim i_1 < i_2$
(ii) $i_1 < i_2 \; \& \; i_2 < i_3 \to i_1 < i_3$
(iii) $i_1 < i_2 \lor i_1 = i_2 \lor i_2 < i_1$

For (i) assume $i_1 < i_2$. By definition there exists $e_1 \in i_1$ and $e_2 \in i_2$ such that $e_1 \sqsubset e_2$. Suppose $i_2 < i_1$. Then there would also exist $e_3 \in i_1$ and $e_4 \in i_2$ such that $e_4 \sqsubset e_3$. Since e_3 and e_1 are both in i_1, by definition of 'instant', $e_3 \; 0 \; e_1$ and, similarly, $e_2 \; 0 \; e_4$. But by (E6) since $e_4 \sqsubset e_3$, $e_3 \; 0 \; e_1$, $e_1 \sqsubset e_2$, we obtain $e_4 \sqsubset e_2$. By (E5) this contradicts $e_4 \; 0 \; e_2$.

For (ii), assume $i_1 < i_2$ and $i_2 < i_3$. It follows, by definition, that there exists $e_1 \in i_1$, $e_2 \in i_2$ such that $e_1 \sqsubset e_2$, and the exists $e_3 \in i_2$ and $e_4 \in i_3$ such that $e_3 \sqsubset e_4$. Since e_2 and e_3 are both in an instant i_2 we also have $e_2 \; 0 \; e_3$. By (E6), $e_1 \sqsubset e_4$. Hence $i_1 < i_3$.

This leaves us to deal with (iii). Assume $i_1 \; i_2$. By definition, there must exist e_1 such that $e_1 \in i_1 - i_2$ or $e_1 \in i_2 - i_1$. We only consider the former possibility since the cases proceed in a similar manner. By definition, there exists an $e_2 \in i_2$ such that $e_1 \; 0 \; e_2$. By (E7) either $e_1 \sqsubset e_2$ or $e_2 \sqsubset e_1$. If the former is true then $i_1 < i_2$; if the latter $i_2 < i_1$.

To impose other constraints on the relation of temporal precedence between instants one has to impose further constraints on the relations between events. For example, for density one must demand the truth of the following.

(E8) $(\forall e_1\, e_2)\,(e_1 < e_2 \rightarrow (\exists e_3)\,(\exists e_4)\,(e_3 < e_2\ \&\ e_1 < e_4\ \&\ e_3\ 0\ e_4))$

Unfortunately, it is difficult to construct a convincing argument for (E8). Indeed, (E8) has little more to recommend it than its analogue (R7).

   Despite this, however, such a theory of events and instants offers a unified view of the two notions and has the laudable advantage of clarifying the relationship between the two in a conceptually satisfying way.

   I believe that the intuitions driving the above account are related to those which led Allen to insist that intervals be taken as primitive. It would be an interesting research topic to see how much of Allen's theory could be reconstructed in terms of the above theory of events and instants.

6.5 TEMPORAL LOGIC, SPECIFICATION AND VERIFICATION

So far we have said nothing about the role of temporal logics in the specification and verification of programs. This is perhaps excusable since this chapter has been directed towards the role of such logics in AI. However, much of the work on specification and verification has been concerned with concurrency and communicating processess, and these issues are of some importance to AI itself. We, therefore, conclude this chapter with two case studies of the use of temporal logics in computer science.

(i) The temporal framework of Manna & Pnueli

Manna & Pnueli (1981) apply temporal logic to the specification and verification of concurrent programs. Their model of time is linear and discrete, and they employ a many-sorted predicate calculus which admits, in addition to the temporal operators discussed in section 6.2, two new ones — Until and Next. The semantics of these operators can be furnished by the following clauses.

$$h(t, \text{Next } A) = 1 \quad \text{iff} \quad h(\text{Succ}(t), A) = 1$$
$$h(t, A \text{ Until } B) = 1 \quad \text{iff} \quad (\exists t' > t)\,(h(t', B) = 1$$
$$\text{and } (\forall t'')\,(t \leqslant t'' \leqslant t')\,(h(t'', A) = 1))$$

where $\text{Succ}(t)$ is the next instant. This makes sense since time is assumed to be discrete.

Before we proceed with some illustrations of the use they make of such a logic we need to briefly describe the style of concurrent programming they employ. Each program has the form

$$P_1 \parallel P_2 \parallel \ldots \parallel P_m$$

where each P_i is a process running in parallel. Each such P_i is an independent transition graph with nodes (locations) labelled from $L_i = \{l_0^i, \ldots, l_e^i\}$ where the sets L_i are taken to be disjoint. The edges (or transitions) in each process are labelled by instructions of the form

$$\underset{a}{\overset{C_a(y) \rightarrow [y := f_a(y)]}{\text{(1)} \longrightarrow \text{(1')}}}$$

where $C_a(y)$ is referred to as the *enabling condition* of the transition a, and f_a is the associated transformation. If $C_a(e)$ is true then the transition a is *enabled* for $y = e$.

For a node l with k outgoing transitions

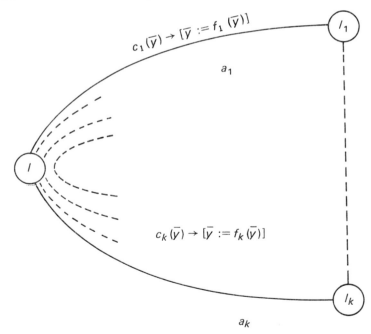

define $E_1(\bar{y}) = C_1(\bar{y}) \vee \ldots \vee c_k(\bar{y})$ to be the *full-exit condition* at node l. The individual conditions are not meant to be exhaustive, thus deadlocks are permitted. The set of program variables $\bar{y} = (y_1, \ldots, y_n)$ is accessible and shared by all the processes.

The following is an example of such a program written in a linear form.

Example To compute the binomial coefficient $\binom{n}{k}$ for integers n and k, such that $0 \leqslant k \leqslant n$.

$$y_1 = n \qquad y_2 = 0 \qquad y_3 = 1$$

l_0 : if $y_1 = (n-k)$ then go to l_e m_0 : if $y_2 = k$ then go to m_e
l_1 : $y_3 := y_3 . y_1$ m_1 : $y_2 := y_2 + 1$
l_2 : $y_1 := y_1 - 1$ m_2 : loop until $y_1 + y_2 \leqslant n$
l_3 : go to l_0 m_3 : $y_3 := y_3 / y_2$
l_e : halt m_e : halt

      – Process $P1$ –   – Process $P2$ –

The computation follows the formula

$$\binom{n}{k} = \frac{n. (n-1). \text{----} . (n + k + l)}{1.2. \text{----} . k}$$

The process P_1 computes the numerator and assigns the value to y_3; the process P_2 computes the denominator and assigns the value to y_2 and then divides y_3 by y_2. The instruction

$$m_2 : \text{loop until } y_1 + y_2 \leqslant n$$

synchronises P_2's operation with P_1 to ensure that y_3 is divided by i only after it has been multiplied by $n - i + 1$. This is to guarantee even divisibility. The Process P_2 thus waits at m_2 until $y_1 + y_2$ is less than or equal to n.

Programs are actually executed using multiprogramming, and so the execution proceeds in a series of discrete steps. Consequently, the problem of fairness arises. The actual scheduler is required to be *fair* in that no process, which is ready to run, will be neglected for ever.

The intention of these authors is to employ temporal logic as a means of reasoning about the execution sequences of such concurrent programs. Consequently, 'time points' are viewed as infinite sequences of states

$$s = s_0, s_1, s_2, \ldots$$

where the relation of temporal precedence between such sequences of states is defined by

$$R\,(s,\,t) =_{\text{def}} (\exists i)\,(t_j = s_{i+j}, j \geqslant 0)$$

that is, the 'later' sequence is to be a prefix of the 'earlier' one. States (or execution states) are actually endowed with a certain structure which contains information about the current locations in the program and the current values of the program variables. More precisely, an execution state $s = \langle \lambda, \bar{e} \rangle$ consists of a vector $\bar{\lambda} = \langle \lambda_1, \ldots, \lambda_m \rangle$, where each $\lambda_i \in L_i$ and λ_i is the node in the transition graph of P_i where execution is to be resumed, and $\bar{e} = \langle e_1, \ldots, e_n \rangle$ is the vector of current values held by the program variables y in the state s.

An *execution sequence* of the program $P = P_1 \| \ldots \| P_m$ is an infinite sequence

$$s_0, s_1, s_2, \ldots$$

of such execution states.

Corresponding to the structure of execution states and sequences, Manna & Pnueli consider temporal formulae which (among others) include the following individual variables

(i)   Local program variables: $y_1, \ldots, y_n$
(ii) Local location variables: $p_1, \ldots, p_m$ which represent the location of each process in a given state. Each p_i ranges over the set L_i.
(iii) Global variables: $x_1, x_2, \ldots, x_n$ where the x_i are input variables.

The notation *atl* is used as an abbreviation for $p_j = l$; where $l \in L_j$. This notation can be naturally extended to a vector of locations.

For a given program P, let $A(\bar{x})$ be a precondition on the input values $\bar{x}$ and let the program variables $\bar{y}$ be initialised to $f_0(\bar{x})$. An execution sequence is then said to be a *(P, A)-initialised computation* if it is a sequence s such that:

(a)   It is a fair execution sequence
(b)   It is properly A-initialised, that is, if $s_0 = \langle \bar{\lambda}, \bar{e} \rangle$ then $\bar{\lambda} = (l_0^1, \ldots, l_0^m)$ and $\bar{e} = f(\bar{x})$ for some $\bar{x}$ such that $A(\bar{x})$.

An execution sequence is said to be a *(P, A)-admissible computation* if it is a suffix of a *(P, A)-initialised* computation. We then define $F(P, A)$ to be the set of all *(P, A)-computations*. A wff is *F(P, A)-valid* if it is true for every sequence in $F(P, A)$. We employ the notation $F(P, A) \models B$ to indicate $F(P, A)$-validity.

We are now in a position to illustrate the expressive power of this language of temporal logic. Manna & Pnueli divide program properties into three groups.

(a)   Invariance properties
(b)   Eventuality properties
(c)   Precedence properties

(a) *Invariance properties*

The first class of properties are those that hold continuously through-out the execution of the program. They are expressible by formulae of the form

$$F(P, A) \vDash A(\bar{x}) \rightarrow GB$$

An example of such a property is *partial correctness*. Let $A(\bar{x})$ be the precondition that restricts the inputs for which the program P is said to be correct, and $B(\bar{x}, \bar{y})$ the statement of correctness. The partial correctness with respect to the specification (A, B) can be expressed as

$$F(P, A) \vDash A(\bar{x}) \rightarrow F(atl_e \rightarrow B(\bar{x}, \bar{y}))$$

where $l_e = (l_e^1, \ldots, l_e^m)$ is the set of terminal locations.

A second example of an invariance property concerns *deadlock freedom*. A concurrent program consisting of m processes is said to be *deadlocked* if no process is enabled. In a deadlock situation each process P_i must be blocked at a location $l \in L_i$ whose full-exit condition is false for the current value $\bar{e}$ of $\bar{y}$. It follows that the only potential deadlock locations are those l for which E_i is not identically true. These are called *waiting* locations. Let $l = (l^1, \ldots, l^m)$ be a tuple of waiting locations, $l^i \in L_j$ not all of which are terminal. Let $E_1, \ldots, E_m$ be their associated full-exit conditions. To prevent deadlock we thus require

$$F(P, A) \vDash A(\bar{x}) \rightarrow G(\bigwedge_{j=1}^{m} atl^j \rightarrow \bigvee_{j=1}^{m} E_j(\bar{y}))$$

In other words, whenever all the processes are each at l^j $(j = 1, \ldots, m)$, at least one of them is enabled.

(b) *Eventuality properties*

These are expressible by wffs of the form

$$F(P, A) \vDash A \rightarrow FB$$

This wff states that for every admissible computation, in which A is initially true, B must be eventually true. An example of this is the following formula which expresses *total correctness*

$$F(P, A) \vDash A(\bar{x}) \rightarrow F(at\bar{l}_e \ \& \ B(\bar{x}, \bar{y}))$$

(c) *Precedence properties*

These are expressed by wffs of the form

$$F(P, A) \vDash A_1 \ \text{Until} \ A_2$$

which expresses the claim that in all admissible computations of P there will be a future instance in which A_2 holds which is such that A_1 will hold until that instance.

(ii) The temporal logic of Halpern, Manna, and Moszkowski

In two recent papers (Halpern, Manna, & Moszkowski (1983), Moszkowski (1983)) these authors have developed an interval based temporal logic which facilitates the rigorous specification and verification of a wide variety of hardware components. Moreover, the temporal logic's applicability appears not to be limited to the task of computer assisted verification and synthesis of circuits. The authors claim that the language, appropriately 'sugared'' could provide a rigorous framework for communicating the behaviour of digital devices (Moszkowski 1983). Indeed, in a forthcoming paper Manna & Moszkowski show how temporal logic can itself be employed as a programming language.

The language of temporal logic that they employ is an extension of the predicate calculus with equality which admits the temporal operator 'Next' and a binary sequencing operator ';'. Once again the model of time they employ is linear and discrete. More precisely, 'time points' are *finite* sequences of states

$$s_0. s_1. s_2. s_3. \ldots . s_n$$

which they refer to as *intervals*.

Models of this language have the form $\langle S, D, I \rangle$ where S is a (non-empty) set of *states*, D a (non-empty) set, and I a mapping which assigns to each variable and interval an element of D, to each (n-place) function symbol and interval an element of $D^n \rightarrow D$, and to each (n-place) relation symbol and interval an element $D^n \rightarrow \{1, 0\}$. The semantic definition of the predicate calculus part of the language is standard, and so we only rehearse the definitions of 'Next' and ';'.

$$h(s_0, \ldots, s_n, \text{Next} A) = 1 \text{ iff } n \geqslant 1 \ \& \ h(s_1, \ldots s_n, A) = 1$$

$$h(s_0. \ldots . s_n, A \ ; B) = 1 \text{ iff } (\exists i) (0 \leqslant i \leqslant n) (h(s_0. \ldots s_i, A) = 1 \ \& \ (h(s_i. \ldots s_n, B) = 1)$$

The semicolon operator thus expresses the sequencing of statements.

Following the authors, we illustrate the expressive power of this language by displaying how certain temporal concepts can be expressed.

(i) *Examining subintervals*

Consider the definition

$$\langle a \rangle\, A =_{\text{def}} (\text{true}\; ;\, A\; ;\, \text{true})$$

$$\boxed{a}\, A =_{\text{def}} \sim \langle a \rangle \sim A$$

A little reflection should convince the reader of the following equivalences:

$$h\,(s_0 \ldots \ldots s_n,\; \langle a \rangle\, A) = 1 \text{ iff } (\exists\, i, j)\,(0 \leqslant i \leqslant j \leqslant n)\,(h\,(s_i \ldots s_j,\, A) = 1)$$

$$h\,(s_0 \ldots \ldots s_n,\; \boxed{a}\, A) = 1 \text{ iff } (\forall\, i, j)\,(0 \leqslant i \leqslant j < n)\,(h\,(s_i \ldots s_j,\, A) = 1)$$

Thus $\langle a \rangle\, A$ is true at $s_0 \ldots s_n$ if A is true on at least one subinterval, and $\boxed{a}\, A$ is true at $s_0 \ldots s_n$ if A is true on every subinterval. Observe that because ';' is associative there is no ambiguity in the definitions.

(ii) *Initial and terminal subintervals*

The operators $\langle i \rangle$ and $\boxed{i}$ are similar to $\langle a \rangle$ and $\boxed{a}$ but examine initial subintervals:

$$\langle i \rangle\, A =_{\text{def}} (\text{true}\; ;\, A)$$

$$\boxed{i}\, A =_{\text{def}} \sim \langle i \rangle \sim A$$

Simiarly, we can define operators which scrutinise terminal subintervals:

$$\langle t \rangle\, A =_{\text{def}} (\text{true}\; ;\, A)$$

$$\boxed{t}\, A =_{\text{def}} \sim \langle t \rangle \sim A$$

(iii) *Initial and final states*

The formula begA tests if A is true in an interval's starting state:

$$\text{beg}A =_{\text{def}} \langle i \rangle\,(\text{empty} \wedge A)$$

where $\text{empty} =_{\text{def}} \sim \text{Next true}$

Correspondingly, finA, given by

$$\text{fin}A =_{\text{def}} \langle t \rangle\,(\text{empty} \vee A)$$

checks whether A holds in the interval's final state.

(iv) *Temporal assignment*
The wff $A \Rightarrow B$ is to be true for an interval if the variable A's initial value equals B's final value.

$$A \Rightarrow B =_{def} (\forall c)\,(\text{beg}(A = c) \rightarrow \text{fin}(B = c))$$

This is referred to as *temporal assignment.*

(v) *The temporal function len*
Timing properties are mangaged by the ue of a 0-place temporal function symbol len where $I(\text{len}, s_0, \ldots, s_n) = n$.

(vi) *Unit delay*
One of the simplest delay devices is modelled by a simple input-output device. The behaviour of such a device can be expressed in terms of intervals by the following predicate:

$$A \text{ del } B =_{def} \boxed{a}\; [(\text{len} = 1) \rightarrow (A \Rightarrow B)]$$

In words, this states that in every subinterval of length exactly one unit, the initial value of the input A equals the final value of the output B.

In the papers cited the authors exhibit a wide range of such devices and thus offer convincing evidence that their language of temporal logic is a useful one for describing and reasoning about hardware circuits.

BIBLIOGRAPHICAL NOTES

McArthur (1979) and Rescher & Urquhart (1971) provide simple introductions to temporal logic. The recent book by Van Benthem is a more up to date text which includes a discussion of event and interval based temporal logics.

The best papers to begin with as regards the application of temporal logics to AI are Allen (1981), Allen and Koomen (1983), and McDermott (1982).

Other relevant contributions to the use of temporal logic in the specification and verification of concurrent programs include Pnueli (1977), Gabbay *et al.* (1980), and Manna & Wolper (1984). These authors apply the propositional temporal logic, essentially in the form discussed in case studies (i) and (ii), to the specification and synthesis of the synchronisation part of communicating processes. They specify and synthesise sychronisation problems within the regime of Hoare's language of Communicating Sequential Processes (CSP).

Allen, J. F. (1981) 'An interval-based representation of temporal knowledge'. *Proc. 7th Int. Joint Conf. on Artificial Intelligence,* Vancouver, Canada, 221–226.

Allen, J. F. & Koomen, J. A. (1983) 'Planning using a temporal world model', *Proc. 8th Int. Joint Conf. on Artificial Intelligence,* ed. A. Bundy, 741–747.

Benthem, J. Van (1983) *The logic of time,* Reidel.

Gabbay, D., Pneuli, A., Shelah, S., & Stain, J. (1980) 'On the temporal logic of programs', *Proc. 18th Symp. on Mathematical Foundations of Computer Science.* Springer Lecture Notes in Computer Science. Vol. 88. ed. Dembinski, 112–152.

Halpern, J., Manna, Z., & Moszkowski, B. (1983) 'A hardware semantics based on temporal intervals', *Proc. 19th Int. Colloqu. on Automata, Languages and Programming.* Springer Lecture Notes in Computer Science. Vol. 54 278–292.

Kamp, J. A. W. (1979) 'Instants and temporal reference', in: A. Von Stechow (ed) *Semantics from different points of view,* Springer Verlag.

Kamp, J. A. W. (1980) 'Some remarks on the logic of change, Part I', in: *Time, tense and quantifiers, Proc.* Stuttgart Conference on the Logic of Tense and Quantification, North Holland. Edited by F. Guenthner.

Kandrashina, E. Yu (1982) 'Representation of temporal knowledge', *Proc. 8th Int. Joint Conf. on Artifical Intelligence (1983).* ed. A. Bundy 346–348.

McArthur, J. (1979) *Tense logic,* Reidel.

McDermott, D. (1982) 'A temporal logic for reasoning about plans and actions', *Cognitive Science* **6** 101–155.

Malik, J. & Binford, T. O. (1983) 'Reasoning in time and space', *Proc. 8th Int. Joint Conf. on Artificial Intelligence (1983).* 343–345.

Manna, Z. & Pneuli, A. (1981) 'Verification of concurrent programs: the temporal framework', in: Boyer, R. S. & Moore, J. S. (eds) *The correctness problem in computer science,* 215–273, Academic Press, New York.

Manna, Z. & Wolper, P. (1984) 'Synthesis of communicating processes from temporal logic', *ACM Trans. on Programming Languages and Systems* **6** (1) 68–93.

Moszkowski, B. (1983) 'A temporal logic for multi-level reasoning about hardware', *Proc. IFIP 6th Int. Symp. on Computer Hardware Description Languages and their Applications, Pittsburgh, Pensylvania, May 1983.*

Moszkowski, B. & Manna, Z. (1983) *Reasoning in interval temporal logic in: Logic of Programs.* Springer Lecture Notes in Computer Science, Vol. 164, 371–381. Ed. Clarke, E. & Kozen, D.

Pnueli, A. (1977) 'The temporal logic of programs', *Proc. IEEE Annual Symposium on Foundations of Computer Science,* Providence R. I. 46–57.

Quine, W. V. O. (1960) *Word and object,* MIT Press.

Rescher, J. & Urquhart, A. (1971) *Temporal logic,* Springer Verlag.

Wiener, N. (1914) 'A contribution to the theory of relative position', *Proc. Cambridge Philosophical Society* 77.

7

Fuzzy logic and expert systems

7.1 FUZZIFICATION

The advocates of fuzzy logic claim that the standard logical formalisms are inadequate in regard to their ability to model informal arguments. So, in this respect at least their motivation is similar to that of the temporal logicians who view classical logic as an inadequate framework in which to express inferences involving temporal notions. However, the change to logic advocated by fuzzy logicians is a great deal more radical. Temporal logicians have extended classical logic to enable it to cope directly with inferences involving some temporalised aspect, so that temporal logic is built upon a foundation of classical logic. The reform advanced by fuzzy logicians cuts much deeper and questions almost every aspect of classical logic itself.

The objective of fuzzy logic is to modify (or 'fuzzify') logic so that it applies directly to informal arguments. Fuzzy logic results from two stages of 'fuzzification':

(i) The introduction of vague predicates into the object language. This results in some form of multivalued logic.
(ii) Treating the metalinguistic predicates 'true' and 'false' as themselves vague or fuzzy.

The second stage is by far the most radical and controversial, and we shall reserve the term *fuzzy logic* for this stage of 'fuzzification.'

Our objective in this chapter is to provide an exposition of the elementary parts of fuzzy set theory and fuzzy logic, and to indicate its applications (both potential and realised) in artificial intelligence generally, but more particularly in expert systems. To begin with we discuss vague predicates and fuzzy sets and develop the elementary parts of fuzzy set theory. We then carry out the first stage of fuzzification by introducing the multi-valued logic of Lukasiewicz. The second stage of fuzzification, namely the introduction of fuzzy truth-values, is discussed in section 4 where we also provide a brief introduction to the topic of 'approximate reasoning'. In section 5 we discuss the application of fuzzy logic to expert systems.

7.2 FUZZY SET THEORY

According to the naive conception of the notion of set, every property determines a set, namely the set of all things which satisfy the property in question. If we identify such properties as functions from some universe of objects U into $\{0, 1\}$ then such properties and subsets of U are formally indistinguishable: any such property P determines a set, $S_P = \{u \in U : P(u) = 1\}$, and conversely any subset S of U generates a property (its membership function) P_s, given by $P_s(u) = 1$ iff $u \in S$.

According to fuzzy set theory, properties and sets also share such an intimate relationship, but the nature of both is fundamentally different from that of their classical counterparts. It is claimed by the devotees of fuzzy-set theory that properties or predicates like *red* and *tall* are vague. For example, it is not always determinate whether a certain person is tall or not. There are some individuals who we would not want to classify as tall or not tall. Such reasoning leads us naturally to some form of 3-valued logic, but fuzzy-set theorists do not stop here. Not only is the borderline between *tall* and *short* (not tall) claimed to be ill-defined, but so are the borderlines between *tall, neither tall nor short,* and *short*. Moreover, it is claimed, this process can be continued ad infinitum: at no point can precise borderlines be set. This leads them to view predicates as functions from U into $[0, 1]$.

What consequences does such a view of predicates have for the nature of sets? Well, fuzzy sets are determined by such predicates as ordinary sets are determined by classical ones. To see how this might work, notice that each classical property P determines the set

$$S_P = \{a : P(a) = 1\}$$

However, where P is a vague predicate the set determined has the following form:

$$\{\langle a, i \rangle : P(a) = i, i \in [0, 1] \}$$

So that fuzzy sets are determined by such vague predicates, and these vague predicates constitute their membership function. For a fuzzy set S we shall write its membership function as U_S. We can no longer view sets just as collections of objects but rather as objects together with an indication of their *grade* of membership.

In classical set theory notions such as subset, union, intersection, and complementation play a crucial role. Each of these operations has a counterpart in the theory of fuzzy sets.

(i) *Subset relation*

When is one fuzzy subset of U to be viewed as a fuzzy subset of a second? Presumably, when the grade of membership of each element, with respect to the second, is at least as good as that of the first. Let A, B be fuzzy subsets of U, then define

$$A \subset B \Leftrightarrow \text{def} \; (\forall u \in U) \, (U_A(u) \leqslant U_B(u))$$

For equality of fuzzy sets we insist that each is a fuzzy subset of the other:

$$A = B \Leftrightarrow \text{def} \; A \subset B \; \& \; B \subset A$$

(ii) *Intersection*

Let A and B be fuzzy subsets of U. Then define the membership function of the intersection of A and B ($A \cap B$) as:

$$U_{A \cap B}(x) = \text{Min} \, (U_A(x), U_B(x))$$

So, for example, if

$$A = \{\langle x1, 0.2 \rangle, \langle x2, 0.7 \rangle, \langle x3, 1 \rangle\} \text{ and}$$
$$B = \{\langle x1, 0.5 \rangle, \langle x2, 0.3 \rangle, \langle x3, 1 \rangle\}$$

then $A \cap B = \{\langle x1, 0.2 \rangle, \langle x2, 0.3 \rangle, \langle x3, 1 \rangle\}$.

(iii) *Union*

Let A and B be fuzzy subsets of U. Then define the membership function of the union of A and B ($A \cup B$) as:

$$U_{A \cup B}(x) = \text{Max} \, (U_A(x), U_B(x)).$$

So in the above example

$$A \cup B = \{\langle x1, 0.5 \rangle, \langle x2, 0.7 \rangle, \langle x3, 1 \rangle\}.$$

(iv) *Complementation*

Let A and B be fuzzy subsets of U. Then we say that A and B are *complementary* iff for each x in U, $U_B(x) = 1 - U_A(x)$. We write $B = \overline{A}$.

All the standard properties of union, intersection, and complementation hold for fuzzy sets (for example, commutativity, associativity, distributivity) except for two notable exceptions:

$$A \cap \overline{A} = \phi$$
$$A \cup \overline{A} = U$$

where ϕ is the set given by $U_\phi(x) = 0$ for each x in U.

This completes our introduction to fuzzy set theory. For more details the reader should consult the literature cited in the bibliograpy.

7.3 MULTI-VALUED LOGIC

The first stage of fuzzification is a consequence of the introduction of fuzzy predicates and relations into the object language. This results in a non-fuzzy multi-valued logic, the so-called *base logic*. We shall illustrate this stage of fuzzification by reference to the MVL of Lukasiewicz. This is obtained by extending the 3-VL of Chapter 3 to a logic in which the truth-values are real numbers in the interval [0, 1]. First, though, we need to extend our concept of partial model.

Definition 3.1 A *multi-valued frame* for L, M, consists of a non-empty set M together with a set of fuzzy relations on M (where a n-place fuzzy relation on M is a function from M^n to [0, 1]).

Such a notion is common to all forms of MVL, but we shall employ it to provide an exposition of the MVL of Lukasiewicz. The logical connectives of his MVL are computed in the following way.

$$
\begin{array}{lll}
\text{(i)} & \neg^{(r)} & = \ 1 - r \\
\text{(ii)} & r1 \wedge r2 & = \ \text{Min}\,(r1, r2) \\
\text{(iii)} & r1 \vee r2 & = \ \text{Max}\,(r1, r2) \\
\text{(iv)} & r1 \rightarrow r2 & = \ \text{Min}\,(1, 1 - r1 + r2) \\
\text{(v)} & \bigwedge_{i \in I} r_i & = \ \underset{i \in I}{\text{Min}}\,(r_i) \\
\text{(vi)} & \bigvee_{i \in I} r_i & = \ \underset{i \in I}{\text{Max}}\,(r_i)
\end{array}
$$

The last two are involved in the specification of unversal and existential quantification respectively. With these logical constants available the semantics for L looks much the same as it did in the 3-valued case.

For convenience we drop all reference to M in what follows.

Let A be a sentence of L. Then we associate with each sentence (closed wff) a real number in $[0, 1]$ as follows:

$$
\begin{aligned}
[C(d'_0, \ldots, d'_{n-1})] &= C^M(d_0, \ldots, d_{n-1}) \\
[A \& B] &= [A] \wedge [B] \\
[\sim A] &= \neg([A]) \\
[A \vee B] &= [A] \vee [B] \\
[A \to B] &= [A] \to [B] \\
[\forall x\, A] &= \bigwedge_{m \in M} [A(m)] \\
[\exists x\, A] &= \bigvee_{m \in M} [A(m)]
\end{aligned}
$$

So that the actual semantic definition is identical in form to the 3-valued logic of Lukasiewicz; the difference is to be located in the definition of the logical constants and opeators.

7.4 FUZZY LOGIC

As already stated, the first stage of fuzzification is a consequence of the introduction of fuzzy predicates into the object language. This results in a non-fuzzy multi-valued logic, the so-called basic logic. The second stage is a great deal more radical and concerns the very notion of truth itself, for at this stage the metalinguistic predicates 'true' and 'false' are themselves treated as fuzzy predicates. Such a move demands not only a complete revision of our concept of truth but also heralds a reappraisal of our traditional understanding of inference and validity.

Zadeh offers two main reasons for adopting fuzzy logic. First, he claims that it avoids the complexities introduced by regimentation of informal argument; secondly, he claims that it is the proper way to acknowledge that 'true' and 'false' are not precise but fuzzy. For the moment we shall not attempt to evaluate these claims but rather adopt a neutral position and attempt to provide a sympathetic and reasonably clear account of the technical aspects of the subject.

In fuzzy logic (FL) the set of truth-values of the base logic, the set of points in the interval $[0, 1]$, is replaced by fuzzy subsets of that set. Zadeh does not, however, allow all fuzzy subsets. This, it is claimed, would result in 'unmanageable complexity'. Instead, Zadeh employs only a countable and structured set of fuzzy subsets of $[0, 1]$ referred to as *linguistic truth-values*. More explicitly, the truth-value set of FL is assumed to be a countable set, TV, of the form

$$TV = \{\text{true, false, not true, very true, not very true,}$$
$$\text{more or less true, rather true, not very true,}$$
$$\text{not very false, ...}\}$$

Each element of this set represents a fuzzy subset of $[0, 1]$. Moreover, each element of TV is 'generated' from the fuzzy set denoted by the term 'true'. So, for example, if U_{true} is the membership function of the fuzzy subset true, then the membership functions for the other members of TV might be given as follows:

$$
\begin{aligned}
U_{\text{false}}(v) &= U_{\text{true}}(1-v) \\
U_{\text{not true}}(v) &= 1 - U_{\text{true}}(v) \\
U_{\text{very true}}(v) &= (U_{\text{true}}(v))^2 \\
U_{\text{rather true}}(v) &= (U_{\text{true}}(v))^{1/2}
\end{aligned}
$$

etc. So that once the meaning of 'true', and the rules of computation are fixed, then so is the meaning of all the members of TV. As a consequence, the meanings of the linguistic truth-values (that is, the fuzzy subsets they denote) is crucially dependent upon the meaning chosen for 'true'. Moreover, it is quite difficult to see such a choice as anything other than arbitrary. Zadeh hints that the choice is motivated by the specific area of discourse under consideration. Consequently, the meanings assigned to the linguistic truth-values are *localised*.

How are the logical constants $\sim$, &, v and $\rightarrow$ to obtain their meanings in a regime where truth values are elements of TV? As a first stab we might proceed as follows:

$$
\begin{aligned}
{[\sim A]}\,(v) &= \neg([A]\,(v)) \\
{[A \,\&\, B]}\,(v) &= [A]\,(v) \wedge [B]\,(v) \\
{[A \vee B]}\,(v) &= [A]\,(v) \vee [B]\,(v) \\
{[A \rightarrow B]}\,(v) &= [A]\,(v) \rightarrow [B]\,(v)
\end{aligned}
$$

where the connectives $\neg$, $\wedge$, $\vee$, $\rightarrow$ are those of the base logic and each $[A]$ denotes a fuzzy subset of $[0, 1]$ represented above by its membership function. But there is a problem with this way of proceeding. We want each sentence in the language to denote not just an arbitrary fuzzy subset of $[0, 1]$ but rather an element of TV. Unfortunately, the above semantics offers no guarantee of this. Zadeh circumvents this difficulty by introducing the notion of a *Linguistic Approximation*. Each fuzzy subset S of $[0, 1]$ has associated with it an element S^* of TV, its so-called *linguistic approximation*.

This is expressed as

$$S^* = \mathrm{LA}(S).$$

Unfortunately, there is not an obvious candidate for the notion of 'best' such approximation, nor a general technique for computing 'good' ones. But whatever the merits of this notion, Zadeh employs it to provide the meanings of the logical constants as follows:

$$[\sim A] \qquad = \qquad \mathrm{LA}(\lambda v. \neg([A] (v)))$$
$$[A \,\&\, B] \qquad = \qquad \mathrm{LA}(\lambda v. ([A] (v) \wedge [B] (v)))$$
$$[A \vee B] \qquad = \qquad \mathrm{LA}(\lambda v. ([A] (v) \vee [B] (v)))$$
$$[A \rightarrow B] \qquad = \qquad \mathrm{LA}(\lambda v. ([A] (v) \rightarrow [B] (v)))$$

where, again, $\neg$, $\wedge$, $\vee$, $\rightarrow$ are the connectives of the base logic. So that now the function [ ] associates with each sentence an element of TV, the set of fuzzy truth-values.

The introduction of fuzzy truth-values paves the way for a rather radical approach to inference. According to Zadeh, inference is only 'approximate'. We now attempt an explication of this notion.

Zadeh illustrates his notion of approximate reasoning by reference to examples of the form

> a is small
> a and b are approximately equal
> _____
> b is more or less small

> Most men are vain
> Socrates is a man
> _____
> It is likely that Socrates is vain

Zadeh views the above examples as special instances of a form of reasoning in which the actual process of inference involves the solution of a system of 'relational assignment equations'. To illustrate what he means by this notion we employ the first example. Consider the statement

> (1) a is small

Under the administration of classical logic this proposition would be rendered true just in case a belongs to the set which constitutes the extension of the predicate small. In fuzzy logic, however, things are somewhat more involved. The predicate small is fuzzy, and proposition

(1) is interpreted as the assignment of a fuzzy predicate as the value of a variable which corresponds to an *implied attribute* of a. More explicitly, (1) would be interpreted as the assignment equation

$$\text{Height}(a) = \text{small}$$

where *Height* is the implied attribute. As a second example consider the second premise of the first inference.

(2) a and b are approximately equal.

In equational terms this would be rendered as

$$(\text{Height}(a), \text{Height}(b)) = \text{approximately equal}$$

where the right-hand side represents a fuzzy subset of $[0, 1] \times [0, 1]$.
    In general, then, a proposition of the form

$$(a_1, \ldots, a_n) \text{ is } C$$

is rendered as the assignment equation

$$R(a_1, \ldots, a_n) = C$$

where R is the implied attribute. For simplicity Zadeh writes this as

$$(a_1, \ldots, a_n) = C$$

The premises of our first inference thus constitute a pair of assignment equations of the form

$$(*) \quad a \quad = \text{small}$$
$$(a, b) = \text{approximately equal}$$

and, in general, a collection of propositions $(ai_1, \ldots, ai_k)$ is Ci, $0 \leqslant i \leqslant n-1$ yield a set of equations $(ai_1, \ldots, ai_k) = Ci, 0 \leqslant i \leqslant n-1$. For Zadeh, approximate inference amounts to 'solving' such systems of equations. As with equations in ordinary algebra, we can solve for any of the variables involved in the equations. We illustrate by solving $(*)$ for the variable b. According to Zadeh's instructions, solving for b yields:

$$b = LA[\text{small} \circ \text{approximately equal}],$$

where $\circ$ is the composition of fuzzy relations, and is given by

$$U_{\text{small} \circ \text{approximately}}(b) =$$

$$\underset{x}{V} [U_{\text{small}}(x) \wedge U_{\text{approximatelyequal}}(x, b)]$$

and where V represents the supremum over all objects in the domain x

of the fuzzy predicate small. Intuitively, the composition of the predicate *small* and the binary relation *approximately equal* represents the fuzzy predicate which returns that value which represents the best fit, between those objects which are in the domain of small, and which are approximately the same height as b. The conclusion

$$b = LA \, [\text{small} \circ \text{approximatelyequal}]$$

thus states, in equational terms, that b is C where C is the linguistic approximation to the fuzzy predicate *small* $\circ$ *approximatelyequal*. We can thus state this so-called compositional rule of inference as follows:

a is A

a and b are B

---

b is $LA \, [A \circ B]$

where A and B are fuzzy relations and $LA \, [A \circ B]$ is a linguistic approximation to their composition.

According to Zadeh & Bellman (1976)

> 'the consequence of a given set of premises depends in an essential way on the meaning attached to the fuzzy sets which appear in the premises'

This is, apparently, a consequence of the local character of fuzzy TV's. Consequently, validity can only be characterised semantically, and the traditional notions of completeness and consistency are 'peripheral' to fuzzy logic.

Following Susan Haack we can summarise the main features of fuzzy logic as follows:

(i) Truth-values are fuzzy;
(ii) The set of linguistic truth-values is not closed under the logical connectives;
(iii) Truth-values are subjective and local;
(iv) Validity can only be characterised semantically (that is, not in terms of axioms and rules of inference);
(v) Completeness, consistency, and axiomatisation are 'peripheral' (Zadeh and Bellman 1976).

In the light of these features it would seem that fuzzy logic is totally lacking in the properties that motivated Frege and Russell to develop modern formal logic. The lack of precise formal rules of inference, the absence and apparent irrelevance of consistency and completeness results, the employment of a philosophically suspect theory of truth; all engender a feeling of insecurity. Indeed, as Haack (1981) points out, fuzzy logic seems hardly recognisable as a 'logic' at all.

Probably, the best defence of fuzzy logic is located not in its conceptual foundations but in its potential applications. After all, many formal frameworks have been employed with much success even though their conceptual foundations have been in a sorry state.

7.5 FUZZY LOGIC AND FUZZY SET THEORY IN EXPERT SYSTEMS

Expert systems are often forced to make judgements in the light of incomplete or unreliable data. The general problem of drawing inferences from uncertain or incomplete data has inspired a variety of technical approaches, one set of which involves some form of fuzzy set theory or fuzzy logic.

One of the earliest approaches to reasoning with uncertainty was incorporated into the MYCIN (Shortliffe 1976) system. It introduced a notion of 'approximate implication' using numbers called 'certainty factors' which were used to indicate the strength of a heuristic rule. For example, MYCIN's knowledge base includes the rule:

If   the infection is primary-bacteremia and
      the site of the culture is one of the sterile sites and
      the suspected portal of entry of the organism is the gastro-
      intestinal tract
then there is suggestive evidence (.7) that the identity of the
      organism is bacteroides.

The number .7 is the certainty factor (in the range 0 to 1) of the conclusion.

In MYCIN, assertions are not just true or false; the reasoning is vague or inexact and is indicated on a numerical scale. Assertions in the knowledge base are represented as 4-tuples which correspond to atomic wff. For example, the assertion 'the identity of organism-2 is Klebsiella with certaintly 0.25' is represented as ⟨IDENTITY ORGANISM-2 KLEBSIELLA .25⟩. MYCIN's conjuction operator performs a minimisation, and its disjunction is furnished with a Bayesian interpretation.

A commonly voiced criticism of such approaches is that they are unnecessarily ad hoc. It is claimed that there are alternative approaches available which are both better documented and understood. Mamdan

& Efstathiou (1982), for example, claim that fuzzy logic itself would provide more secure foundation for the enterprise.

As a matter of fact, PROSPECTOR already employs some form of fuzzy set theory, at least according to the recent account given by Gaschnig (1982). PROSPECTOR is a system developed by R. Duda, P. Hart, and others at SRI in Palo Alto, California. Its objective is to aid geologists to assess the suitability of a given region as a site for the mining of ore deposits of various types. The program's knowledge of a particular ore deposit is stored in the form of an 'inference network' of *relations* between field evidence and geological hypotheses There are three kinds of relation used in the inference network: (i) logical relations, (ii) plausible relations, and (iii) contextual relations. The application of fuzzy set theory is to be found in relations of type (i). The truth-value of assertions are indicated only on a numerical scale. The designers of PROSPECTOR employed fuzzy-set formulae to determine the truth-value of hypotheses involving the logical connectives.

Zadeh himself (1981) has developed what he refers to as a meaning representation language called PROF. PROF has data types whose task is to represent the meaning of natural language sentences. These data types possess the overall structure of objects which are defined by their attributes, but whose values are given as a possibility distribution on the whole space of relevant values. It is basically an extension of the relational data base model, and seems to possess some affinities to the frames approach to knowledge based systems. Kohout & Bandler (1982) survey the use of fuzzy many-valued logics in existing expert systems, and they outline a new framework for the design of fuzzy expert systems. Formally, their approach is based on many-valued extensions of relational algebras. The data-base of their proposed expert system uses a fuzzy relational model. They argue that the available implementations of relational data-bases are in terms of 'hard' static deterministic relations, whereas in real-world applications data is often incomplete, imprecise, inherently dynamic, and non-deterministic.

Other applications of fuzzy logic and fuzzy set theory to expert systems and diagnosis can be found, for example, in Lesmo, Saitta, & Torasso (1983), Whalen & Schott (1981), Martin-Clouaire (1982), and Soula & Sanchez (1982).

In a recent paper, Prade (1983) offers a review of different approximate reasoning techniques which have been proposed for dealing with uncertain or imprecise knowledge in expert systems. In this paper he considers the belief theory of Shefer (1976) Zadeh's possibility theory (Zadeh 1981), Bayesian inference as well as the more empirical proposals to be found in MYCIN and PROSPECTOR. This paper is a good starting point for someone interested in the type of reasoning employed in expert systems. It also contains a rather extensive bibliography. In this regard the paper of Friedman (1983) is also worthy of attention.

Keravnou (1983) surveys most of the existing expert systems, paying particular attention to the various forms of inference employed.

Whatever the conceptual merits of fuzzy set theory and fuzzy logic, they appear to be playing a rather influential, if controversial, role in the development of expert systems.

In conclusion, it is worth pointing out that many authors employ the term 'fuzzy logic' for any form of inference which involves some notion of vagueness. For example, many expert systems employ some form of numerical assignment to assertions which are often combined in ways which suggest that such assignments behave mathematically like probabilities. The term 'fuzzy logic' has a reasonably clear meaning in the works of Zadeh and his disciples, and should not be confused with the more general and vague ideas which are to be found in the more unsophisticated expert systems literature.

BIBLIOGRAPHICAL NOTES

We have only scratched the surface of the whole area of fuzzy set theory and fuzzy logic. We hope to have provided an elementary and accessible introduction to the area, but the interested reader can do no better than consult the original papers of Zadeh, in particular Zadeh (1965a) and Zadeh (1975b). Gaines (1977) is a survey of the whole area of fuzzy systems and is a good starting point for the student of fuzzy systems. This paper contains an extensive bibliography of the whole area up to 1977.

As regards expert systems itself, the book edited by Michie (1983) contains a useful collection of introductory papers.

Friedman, L. (1983) 'Extended plausible inference', *Proc. 7th Int. Joint Conf. on Artificial Intelligence (1983)* 487–495.

Gaines, B. R. (1977) 'Foundations of fuzzy reasoning' in: *J. Man-Machine Studies* 8 623–668.

Gaschnig, J. (1982) 'PROSPECTOR: an expert system for mineral exploration' in: *Introductory readings in Expert Systems,* D. Michie (ed), Gordon & Breach 47–65.

Haack, S. (1981) *The philosophy of logics,* Cambridge University Press.

Keravnou, E. (1983) 'Survey of selected expert systems', MSc dissertation, Brunel University.

Kohout, L. J. U. & Bandler, W. (1982) 'Fuzzy expert systems' in: *Proc. 1982 ACM Symp. on Expert Systems,* Brunel University 1982.

Lesmo, L., Saitta, L. & Torasso, P. (1983) 'Fuzzy production rules: a learning methodology', in: *Advances in fuzzy set theory and applications* P. P. Wang (ed), Plenum Press.

Mamdan, E. H. & Efstathiou, J. (1982) 'Fuzzy logic' in: *Proc. 1982 ACM Symp. on Expert Systems,* Brunel University 1982.

Martin-Clouaire, R. (1982) 'A computer-aided medical diagnosis method based on a fuzzy set theoretical approach'. MSc Thesis, University of Saskatchewan.

Michie, D. (1983) *Introductory readings in expert systems* Gordon & Breach.

Prade, H. (1983) 'A synthetic view of approximate reasoning', in: *Proc. 8th Int. Joint Conf. on Artificial Intelligence (1983).* 130–136.

Shefer, G. (1976) *A mathematical theory of evidence,* Princeton University Press.

Shortliffe, E. H. (1976) *Computer-based medical consultations: MYCIN,* Elsevier, New York.

Soula, G. & Sanchez, E. (1982) 'Soft deduction rules in medical diagnosis processes' in: *Approximate reasoning in decision analysis,* Gupta, M. M. & Sanchez, E. (eds), North-Holland 77–88.

Whalen, T. & Schott, B. (1981) 'Fuzzy production systems for decision support' in: *Proc. Int. Conf. on Cybernetics and Society, Atlanta* 649–653.

Zadeh, L. A. (1965) 'Fuzzy sets' *Inform. & Control* 8 338–353.

Zadeh, L. A. (1974) '"Fuzzy logic" and its application to approximate reasoning', in: *Information Processing 74, Proc. IFIP Congress 74,* Amsterdam, North-Holland, 591–594.

Zadeh, L. A. (1975) 'Fuzzy logic and approximate reasoning', *Synthese* 30 407–428.

Zadeh, L. A. (1976) 'Semantic inference from fuzzy premises' in: *Proc. 6th Int. Symp. on Multiple-Valued Logic, I.E.E.E. 76CH1111-4C, May,* 217–218.

Zadeh, L. A. & Bellman, (1976) 'Local and fuzzy logics', *Memorandum No. ERL-M584,* Electronics Research Lab., Berkeley, California

Zadeh, L. A. (1976b) 'A fuzzy-algorithmic approach to the definition of complex or imprecise concepts' in: *Int. Jour. Man-Machine Studies* 8 249–291.

Zadeh, L. A. (1976c) 'A fuzzy-algorithmic approach to the definition of complex or imprecise concepts', Bossel, H. Klaczko, S. & Muller, N. (eds) *Systems theory in the social sciences,* Basel, Birkhauser Verlag 202–282.
Zadeh, L. A. (1981) 'PROF – a meaning representation language for natural languages' in *Fuzzy reasoning and its applications,* Mamdani, E. H. & Gaines, B. R. (eds), Academic Press.

8

Other logics and future prospects

Many areas of non-standard Logic have been ignored in our presentation. This is not because we undervalue their potential importance as possible tools in AI research. Obviously, in a text such as this some selection has to be made, and we have chosen to study logics which have been taken up by the AI and computer science community as being of some immediate usefulness. In this chapter we briefly review some of the logics which we have so far ignored. We then conclude with a somewhat personal view of the whole area and the prospects for future work.

8.1 OTHER LOGICS

(i) Many-sorted logics

Two-sorted predicate logic differs from ordinary first-order logic in that it admits two distinct sorts of variable. Moreover, function symbols and relation symbols are sorted in the sense that their argument places are restricted to terms of the appropriate sort. For example, the binary relation *motherof* might be permitted only to take objects of sort *female* in its first argument place and arguments of sort *human* in its second.

Such logics have been employed in many AI applications. In particular, the logics utilised in the case studies of Chapter 6 admit variables of sort *instants, events,* and *actions.*

Model structures for two-sorted logic employ two domains D_s, $D_{s'}$ with sorted functions and relations operating on these domains. For example, a relation of sort $s \times s'$ would be a subset of $D_s \times D_{s'}$.

Two-sorted predicate logic is only superficially stronger than ordinary logic, although it often facilitates a more natural expression of the intuitions. Such logics can be easily reduced to standard logic by forming the union of the sorted domains $D_s \cup D_{s'}$ and introducing new binary predicates P_s and $P_{s'}$ to sort out the different sorts of elements. This reduction permits many of the results of first-order logic to be lifted to the many-sorted case. For a good introduction see Feferman (1974).

(ii) Weak second-order logic

This is an attempt to build the notion of *finite* into logic in a natural way. Consider a first-order language L with variables $x, y, z, \ldots$. Let L^* be the two-sorted language obtained from L by the addition of the new class of variables $a, b, c, \ldots$ and a membership symbol '$\in$'. A model structure for L^* can be obtained from a model structure $M = \langle M, -- \rangle$ for L as follows: Define

$$HF_0(M) = \emptyset$$
$$HF_{n+1}(M) = \{\text{all finite subsets of } M \cup HF_n(M)\}$$
$$HF(M) = \bigcup_n HF_n(M)$$

Then define

$$HF(M) = \langle M, HF(M), \in \restriction (M \cup HF(M)) \rangle$$

$HF(M)$ is called the structure of *hereditary finite sets* on M. In weak second-order logic we employ wffs of L^* where the set variables $a, b, c, \ldots$ range over $HF(M)$.

This logic facilitates the expression of properties of integers, finite sets, finite sequences, etc. in a rather natural way.

Given the sort of discrete structures employed in computer science and AI, weak-second logic may turn out to be a rather natural logic for many computer science applications.

(iii) Infinitary logic

Whereas weak second-order logic attempts to incorporate the notion of finite into the semantics, infinitary logic does it through the syntax. This is achieved by allowing infinite conjuctions and disjunctions. For example,

$$(\forall x)\,[x = a \lor 2x = a \lor \ldots\,].$$

The logic $L_{\omega_1,\omega}$ admits wff of the form $\underset{i \geqslant 0}{\bigwedge}\; A_i,\; \underset{i \geqslant 0}{\bigvee}\; A_i$ (respectively infinite conjunctions and disjunctions).

Engeler (1967) suggests the use of infinitary logic as a logic for programming.

8.2 PROSPECTS

In one way or another we have discussed, albeit however briefly, most logics which come under the banner of non-standard logics. In Chapter 2 we developed modal logic and discussed applications of it to computer science; in Chapter 3 we looked at three-valued logics and their computational interpretations; in Chapter 4 we studied intuitionistic logic and discussed one application of it to computer science. In Chapter 5 we utilised each of these non-standard logics in developing various theories of non-monotonic inference. In Chapter 6 we investigated the applications of temporal logic to AI, and in Chapter 7 the application of fuzzy logic to expert systems.

None of these applications is in any sense definitive. Most are controversial and tentative. Nevertheless, the power of non-standard logics in computer science generally, and more particularly in AI, has, I believe, been demonstrated. Much is known about many of these topics, and they provide the AI researcher with precise and formal tools with which to develop theories of knowledge representation and plausible inference. My belief is that the use of such logics in AI will become a very common place phenomenon.

In particular, the increased use of some form of temporal logic seems quite likely. No doubt AI workers will have to develop temporal logics appropriate to their particular domains of application. In this regard the current developments of event logics may provide some inspiration. There appears to be a clear need to reason about events and actions; and some type of logic geared to reason about such, therefore seems required.

So far, intuitionistic logic has found little direct application in AI. If, however, the Martin-Löf school is correct about the tight relationship which exists between intuitionistic logic and computer science, then AI itself is surely going to be influenced.

As regards the general application of the work on specification and verification to AI much can be said, but I will settle for stating one general opinion. Many AI programs are an attempt to develop a theory of some description (for example, a theory of visual perception or natural language understanding). Often, however, such programs conflate two separate issues. The program not only incorporates the theory itself but also the details of a specific implementation. Indeed, in many cases the two parts are so tightly bound together that a conceptual separation is impossible. It is precisely here that an implementation-independent specification of the theory would be so valuable. It would greatly facilitate the task of comparing competing AI theories. It is often hard to evaluate the merits or otherwise of the theory because the details of the implementation get in the way. The methodology of specification, program development, and verification which has become a central part of main stream computer science, might well provide some guidelines to the AI worker.

Throughout the text, much emphasis has been placed upon the semantic interpretation of the various logics considered. In Chapter 2 modal logic was introduced, and the interpretation of the modal operators M and L was furnished by the notion of possible world. Our raw intuitions were educated and sharpened through the actual semantic definition. In Chapter 3 we developed 3-valued logics, and once again used the notion of a partial model to provide a precise formulation of our intuitive mumblings. The approach to non-monotonic inference in Chapter 5 was predominately semantic. Each of the theories of non-montonic inference was introduced via some pre-theoretical intuitions, and the formal theories were sub-sequently developed in accord with such. In the development of temporal logics in Chapter 6, we again attempted to motivate the logics from a semantic perspective where the basic model structures related to our intuitive conceptions of time and temporal precedence.

Such an approach to logic and its applications is not an arid academic exercise. Our pre-theoretical intuitions can often be ill-formed and misleading. The enterprise of providing a formal semantic definition often strengthens our grasp of the underlying intuitions by providing a precise formulation. Of course, it may turn out that our first attempts at formalisation do not quite capture our underlying intuitions. But it is precisely here that the power of formal semantics is most readily seen. Once we have a precise semantic theory we can measure it against our intuitions and if need be modify it if found inadequate. Moreover, such a formal theory provides a background and yardstick for axiomatisation. We require an axiomatisation which is both sound and complete, and such notions have no precise sense outside of a fully developed semantic theory.

All this is common ground to the logician, so why make such a fuss about the issue here? The reason is simple: the message has not been understood and accepted by most AI workers. Indeed, often very little attempt is made to justify their formalisms from any sort of semantic perspective. My hope is that this state of affairs will be short-lived.

BIBLIOGRAPHY

Engler, E. 'Algorithmic properties of structures', *Mathematical Systems Theory* 1 1967 183–195.

Feferman, S. (1974) 'Applications of many-sorted interpolation theorems', in: *Proc. Tarski Symp. (American Mathematical Society, Providence, R.I.)* 102–148.

Index

Accessibility, 19
Approximate Reasoning, 107
Autoepistemic Model, 73
Autoepistemic Theory, 74

Bochvar Logic, 35

Canonical Types, 51
Classical Logic, 14, 15, 16
Completeness, 16
Continuity, 83

Default Reasoning, 67
Density, 82
Dynamic Logic, 25

Elimination Rules, 52
Evaluation, 50
Events, 84, 87
Event Structures, 90, 91
External Connectives, 36

Fixed-Point Theorem, 39
Fuzzification, 101
Fuzzy Sets, 102, 103

Gabbay Structure, 65

Infinitary Logic, 116
Instants, 90
Intervals, 96
Introduction Rules, 51
Intuitionism, 44

Judgements, 50, 51

Kleene Logics, 33, 34

Linguistic Approximation, 106
Linearity, 81, 82
Local Truth Values, 106, 109
Lukasiewicz Logic, 34

Many-Sorted Logic, 115
Modal Frame, 19
Monotonicity, 37
MYCIN, 110

Necessity Operator, 19

Partial Correctness, 26
Possible Worlds, 19, 20
Possibilitation Rule, 63
Possibility Operator, 19
PROSPECTOR, 111
Proof Rules, 45, 46, 47

Saturated Expression, 48
Second-Order Logic, 116
Specifications, 53
Stores, 23
Strictness, 40

Temporal Frame, 80
Time Points, 80
Truth-Value Gaps, 32
Types, 48